TAXATION, GOVERNMENT SPENDING AND ECONOMIC GROWTH

EDITED BY PHILIP BOOTH

with contributions from

RYAN BOURNE

RORY MEAKIN

LUCY MINFORD

PATRICK MINFORD

DAVID B. SMITH

Institute of
Economic Affairs

First published in Great Britain in 2016 by
The Institute of Economic Affairs
2 Lord North Street
Westminster
London SW1P 3LB
in association with London Publishing Partnership Ltd
www.londonpublishingpartnership.co.uk

The mission of the Institute of Economic Affairs is to improve understanding of the
fundamental institutions of a free society by analysing and expounding the role of
markets in solving economic and social problems.

A CIP catalogue record for this book is available from the British Library.

ISBN 978-0-255-36734-9

Many IEA publications are translated into languages other
than English or are reprinted. Permission to translate or to reprint
should be sought from the Director General at the address above.

Typeset in Kepler by T&T Productions Ltd
www.tandtproductions.com

Printed and bound in Great Britain by Page Bros

Taxation, Government Spending and Economic Growth

CONTENTS

THE AUTHORS

Philip Booth

Philip Booth is Academic and Research Director at the Institute of Economic Affairs and Professor of Finance, Public Policy and Ethics at St Mary's University, Twickenham. From 1 November 2016, he will be Director of Research and Public Engagement at St Mary's. Previously, he worked for the Bank of England as an advisor on financial stability issues and has been Associate Dean of Cass Business School. He has written widely, including a number of books, on investment, finance, social insurance and pensions as well as on the relationship between Catholic social teaching and economics. Philip has a BA in economics from the University of Durham and a PhD from City University.

Ryan Bourne

Ryan Bourne is Head of Public Policy at the IEA and a weekly columnist for *CityAM*. He has previously worked at both the Centre for Policy Studies and Frontier Economics, and has written widely on economic topics.

Rory Meakin

Rory Meakin is a research fellow at the TaxPayers' Alliance, where he was previously Head of Tax Policy and Research Director. He was lead researcher to their joint project with the Institute of Directors, the 2020 Tax Commission.

Lucy Minford

Lucy Minford is currently a postdoctoral research fellow in economics at Cardiff Business School. Her doctoral research was funded by the UK Economic and Social Research Council, and she obtained her PhD in economics from Cardiff University in 2015. Her research interests lie in economic growth and applied macroeconomics. In addition to her economics training, Lucy has a BA in Classics from Magdalen College, Oxford.

Patrick Minford

Patrick Minford is Professor of Economics at Cardiff University, where he directs the Julian Hodge Institute of Applied Macroeconomics. His main research interest is in macroeconomic modelling and forecasting. Between 1967 and 1976 he held a variety of economic positions, including spells in East Africa, industry, HM Treasury and its delegation in Washington, DC. From 1976 to 1997, he was the Edward Gonner Professor of Applied Economics at Liverpool University, where he founded and directed the Liverpool Research Group in Macroeconomics; this built the 'Liverpool Model' of the UK, which was influential in forecasting and policy analysis during the 1980s. During the 1990s he also undertook part-time roles in the UK administration: he was a Member of the Monopolies and Mergers Commission from 1990 to 1996, and one of HM Treasury's Panel of Forecasters ('Wise Men/Persons') from 1993 to 1996. He was made a CBE in 1996. His published work includes books, journal articles and op-ed pieces in the area of macroeconomics and related policy issues.

David B. Smith

David B. Smith studied economics at Trinity College, Cambridge, and the University of Essex before working as a macroeconomic modeller and economic forecaster, predominantly in banks and security houses, from 1968 to 2006. He was also a Visiting Professor at the University of Derby from 2006 to 2014 and Chairman of the IEA's Shadow Monetary Policy Committee between 2003 and 2014. David has published numerous papers on topics such as fiscal policy, monetary issues and financial regulation since the mid 1970s. His IEA monograph *Living with Leviathan: Public Spending, Taxes and Economic Performance* gained the IEA's Arthur Seldon Award for excellence in 2007.

FOREWORD

Views about the effect of the burden of taxation and government spending on economic growth and welfare differ sharply between classical liberals and social democrats. The social democrat belief, that welfare can be improved by taking resources from one group of people and giving them to another or by providing goods and services to the population that are financed by taxation, is at odds with the classical liberal view that spending decisions are best made by individuals who can, as Hayek would say, discover the most valuable ways to serve one another.

One of the greatest problems in the debate is the implicit assumption that the actions of government in increasing taxation and government spending are a zero sum game – one group benefits and another (less-deserving) group loses. The idea that there may be welfare losses and that those welfare losses may be so large that everybody loses out from increasing government spending is rarely entertained.

This problem is exacerbated by a lack of reliable data and statistical analyses which show the burdens of government spending and taxation on economic growth.

The authors of this monograph have taken a rigorous and data-driven approach to discovering and documenting the size of the state and how government spending and regulation affect the wider economy. But, most importantly, they have undertaken a major and original statistical analysis of the economic costs of high taxes and, equally importantly, which taxes cause the most economic harm.

This book is therefore a vital and timely addition to the economic debate, particularly coming as even the mild and begrudging efforts at fiscal consolidation from the previous coalition and Conservative governments appear to be at risk of reversal.

As the opening section of the book points out, while the state has undoubtedly grown vastly since the dawn of the twentieth century, measuring its growth is plagued with technical and accounting issues. David B. Smith explains the difficulty of even getting true facts and figures on government spending – and how often the debate on tax and spending figures has been based on statistics that are subsequently invalidated or retrospectively changed.

But, even once these are accounted for, the efforts of the coalition and Conservative governments to impose so-called 'austerity' on the public finances were exaggerated and subject to historical error. Leaving aside changes in national accounting conventions which have made true and robust comparisons difficult, the small scale of real spending consolidation means that attempts to claim, as some have, that cuts are returning Britain to the world of *The Road to Wigan Pier* are simply wrong.

Having identified the problem with existing statistics, in the second section of the monograph Patrick Minford and Lucy Minford, in separate contributions, examine the possible economic benefits from cutting the size of the state – particularly cutting the tax burden – and also develop robust new techniques for identifying the real effect that government intervention has on the wider economy.

Having determined the level of taxation and government spending that is appropriate, the next question that needs to be considered is how to raise the required tax revenues. The final section of the monograph, Chapters 9–11 by Rory Meakin, is nothing less than a full blueprint for an effective, fair, liberal and welfare-maximising taxation policy. The UK's current tax system is a very long way from the ideal. The author of this section identifies twenty current taxes that should be abolished, and presents a reformed tax system to raise 20–25 per cent of national income from five main forms of tax: income tax, VAT, a housing consumption tax, a land-value tax and fuel duty.

With the UK currently in a state of political and policy upheaval, with a new ministerial team in office and the economic opportunities (and risks) of Brexit in the near future, this monograph is an exciting and radical piece that charts both why taxes and government spending must be cut and the tax system changed beyond all recognition. The knowledge and expertise of the authors, not to mention the statistical analysis and original research that this work includes, means this monograph deserves close attention from anyone with an interest in the size of the state or the taxation system.

MARK LITTLEWOOD
Director General and Ralph Harris Fellow
Institute of Economic Affairs
October 2016

The views expressed in this monograph are, as in all IEA publications, those of the authors and not those of the Institute (which has no corporate view), its managing trustees, Academic Advisory Council members or senior staff. With some exceptions, such as with the publication of lectures, all IEA monographs are blind peer-reviewed by at least two academics or researchers who are experts in the field.

SUMMARY

- Measuring taxation and government spending as a proportion of national income is beset with difficulties. However, it is clear that there has been a strong upward trend in taxation and government spending as a proportion of national income in the developed countries over the last 100 years. At the beginning of World War I, the UK government spent just over one eighth of national income; now it spends between 40 per cent and slightly over 45 per cent (depending on how national income is measured).

- Government spending as a proportion of national income in the UK is at a similar level to that in Germany but is considerably higher than in Switzerland, Australia and Ireland. Government spending is also somewhat higher in the UK than in Canada, the US and New Zealand. Thus, it is clear that a welfare state of significant size can be provided at levels of government spending far below those in the UK. It is also notable that, in some UK regions, government spending is between two thirds and three quarters of regional GDP, depending on the definition employed.

- It is government spending rather than taxation that ultimately determines the total burden of government activity on the private sector. Although government spending can be financed by borrowing or creating inflation, all government spending is normally a call on resources that have alternative uses or involves transfers from one group in society to another. If a government borrows money, this has to be financed at the time of borrowing and then serviced by future generations of taxpayers.

- Although there is a general perception that there has been a significant reduction in government spending since 2010, there has not been. Nominal spending increased by 4.6 per cent in total between 2010 and 2015 and real spending fell by just 0.5 per cent a year. Real spending per capita fell by a little more – about 1 per cent per year. By 2015, government spending remained at over 45 per cent of GDP (at factor cost). Over the five years to 2020, nominal government spending is planned to continue to rise, real government spending to go up slightly and spending as a proportion of national income at factor cost fall to 41 per cent.

- Some forms of government spending can promote growth, especially capital spending. However, this does not mean that the resources concerned might not be better employed elsewhere, including for supply-side enhancing tax cuts. Spending on government consumption tends to harm growth. Spending on badly designed transfer payment systems can be especially damaging as they can reduce work incentives. Despite rising government spending in general, there has been a fall in spending on investment while there has been a huge rise in spending on government consumption and transfer payments. Government spending on investment is extremely volatile, but, by way of example, it has fallen from over 6 per cent of national income in the late 1960s to less than 3 per cent today. Welfare payments have almost doubled over the same period as a percentage of national income to their current levels of around 14 per cent (this excludes health and education spending). Even during the period 2010–15, there was a significant reorientation of spending. Public order and safety (comprising much of the 'nightwatchman' functions of the state) had reductions in real spending of about 15 per cent while transport saw cuts of 10 per cent. Meanwhile, spending on both health and social protection increased in real terms. These trends will not be reversed and may be further reinforced in the years to 2020.

- The taxes that have to be raised to finance government spending damage growth through a number of channels. These include reduced incentives for work and saving and reduced incentives for entrepreneurship. Over the last three decades a considerable amount of evidence has been amassed that suggests that tax has a significant negative impact on growth. This evidence suggests that a 10 percentage point increase in the tax or government spending burden is associated with approximately a 1 per cent fall in the growth rate in the long term. The negative impact of tax on growth is also far greater than the benefits to growth that might arise from increased government spending, even if that spending is on investment or subsidising private sector research and development. There are, however, problems with the 'growth regression' approach that generates these results. For example, they cannot necessarily distinguish between cause and effect.
- In many ways, regulation and tax are substitutes for each other and have similar effects. For example, politicians can attempt to improve living standards by regulating wages and other working conditions or by providing in-work welfare benefits. Robust new modelling has been undertaken as part of the research for this project on the impact of tax and regulation on productivity. This modelling is not subject to the problems of the earlier tax and growth studies. This research finds that a 10 percentage point fall in a combined index of top marginal tax rates and regulation relative to its trend produces a rise in output over about thirty years of 24 per cent. This

is equivalent to an increase in the growth rate over the thirty years following the cut of about 0.8 percentage points per annum. The model does not distinguish between regulation and tax. However, the model uses data from a period in which falls in marginal tax rates have been much more frequent than changes in regulation. As such, it is reasonable to infer that a 10 percentage point cut in the top marginal tax rate would bring about the improvement in growth indicated by the model.

- In theory at least, we can identify a growth-maximising, a welfare-maximising and a revenue-maximising share of taxation in national income. The last of these points is the 'top' of the Laffer curve – that is, the point at which, if the government tries to raise more in taxation, the negative effects of taxation on growth are so great that tax revenue is actually reduced. The maximum sustainable level of government spending is a little different from this as a result of the existence of non-tax-based government revenue and the complications of debt dynamics. The welfare-maximising share of taxation in national income is greater than the growth-maximising share because there may be some functions that increase welfare while reducing measured economic growth.

- The growth-maximising share of government spending in GDP is probably in the range 18.5–23.5 per cent of national income, using current (July 2016) UK definitions at market prices. The welfare-maximising share is probably in the range 26.5–32.5 per cent of national income. The maximum sustainable level of government spending is probably in the range 37–38 per cent of national income. Even on the projections set out in the March 2016 Budget and without any relaxation of the purse strings, government spending will only just come down to sustainable levels by 2020/21.

- All taxes do not affect growth in the same way. For example, taxes on mobile capital and high marginal rates of tax on income affect growth disproportionately. Taxes on land, consumption and on economic activities that lead to harmful 'spillover' effects reduce growth to a lesser extent and can even improve economic welfare.
- The overall design of the tax system also affects economic growth. Ideally, a tax system should have low negative effects on welfare and economic efficiency; low administration and compliance costs; fair and non-discriminatory procedures in the way companies and individuals are treated; and be transparent and easily understandable. The UK system is a long way from meeting these goals.
- More specifically, tax systems should be designed so that there is a broad understanding of the basic facts of who pays how much, with simple rules, thresholds, schedules and rates. Tax should be codified so that taxpayers know what is expected and can arrange their affairs accordingly with any ambiguity kept to a minimum. To facilitate this, a formal tax strategy should be adopted by the government, with changes announced in advance and with explanations of how each change helps bring the system closer to implementing the overall strategy.
- The UK has a very badly designed tax system with high marginal rates, huge complexity, taxes that discourage wealth-creating economic activity and wide-ranging exemptions. Current property taxes provide a good example of how badly our tax system is designed. These taxes raise nearly 4 per cent of national income. Council tax is based on a complex system of thresholds and is, in fact, regressive, at least in part. Stamp duty land tax artificially depresses property values, discourages investment and distorts the allocation of assets – for example, by discouraging older

people from moving to smaller accommodation when they no longer need as much space. Current property taxes should be abolished and replaced with taxes that damage economic welfare to a much lesser degree.

- Overall, the UK government should abolish twenty current taxes. Among other taxes, corporation tax, national insurance, capital gains tax, inheritance tax, council tax, business rates, the television licence fee, the apprenticeship levy, stamp duties, alcohol duties, tobacco duties, vehicle excise duty and air passenger duty should be abolished. A radically reformed tax system should be designed to raise around 20–25 per cent of national income. It would comprise the following main elements:
  - A flat-rate income tax set at 15 per cent of income above a personal allowance of around £10,000. Distributed corporate profits would also be taxed at this rate.
  - VAT set at 12.5 per cent, with most exemptions abolished.
  - A new housing consumption tax on rents and imputed rents to mimic VAT at 12.5 per cent.
  - A new location land-value tax.
  - Fuel duty retained at around half the current rate.
- If this package were implemented, static modelling would suggest that the poorest decile would enjoy tax cuts worth 26 per cent of gross income, followed by 19 per cent, 17 per cent and then 13 per cent for the fourth poorest decile before further falling to 7 per cent for the fourth richest decile. The benefit of the proposed tax changes then rises slightly with income.
- Because lower taxes would lead to higher growth and because there would be a tax system that led to far fewer distortions of economic decisions, it is likely that employment, productivity and wage levels would rise considerably. These effects are likely to disproportionately

benefit the poor as they are more likely to be at the margins of the labour market in insecure, low-paid employment or unemployed.

- Tax policy should be formulated to increase certainty, stability and transparency. The government should set out a formal tax strategy that expresses its medium-term and long-term intentions. Tax policy decision-making should be taken out of annual budgets and implemented separately from periodic statements involving economic and fiscal forecasting so that fuller attention can be devoted to the implications of both tax policy changes and changes in budgetary and economic forecasts, respectively.

TABLES, FIGURES AND BOXES

1 INTRODUCTION

Philip Booth

The growth of government spending

The measurement of national income and government spending is perhaps surprisingly controversial. An indication of the difficulties was given in the wake of the government's 2014 Budget when one BBC commentator suggested that planned reductions in government spending as a proportion of national income would take us back to the days of *The Road to Wigan Pier* (that is, to the 1930s). More careful analysis of definitions of national income and the different categories of government spending demonstrated that this assertion was a long way wide of the mark – indeed, it was absurd.

Analysis of the data shows that since the beginning of the twentieth century there has been a huge growth in government spending. This growth has varied somewhat across countries, but the pattern has been remarkably consistent.

So, what can we say about government spending over time? Table 1 shows government spending as a proportion of national income for six countries since 1870 and is a summary of Table 7 in Part 1. In the UK, government spending has grown from around 10 per cent of national income at the beginning of the twentieth century to somewhat over 40 per cent today. There were big jumps in spending during the two world wars.

The trends in the other countries are similar. It is notable that in the US, often regarded as different from other countries,

Table 1   Ratios of general government expenditure, including transfers, to money GDP at market prices (%) – selected countries

	1870	1913	1920	1937	1960	1980	2000	2010	2015
Australia	18.3	16.5	19.3	14.8	21.2	34.1	34.6	36.6	35.6
France	12.6	17.0	27.6	29.0	34.6	46.1	51.1	56.4	57.0
Germany	10.0	14.8	25.0	34.1	32.4	47.9	44.7	47.4	44.0
UK	9.4	12.7	26.2	30.0	32.2	44.7	37.8	48.8	43.2
USA	7.3	7.5	12.1	19.4	30.0	35.3	33.9	43.2	37.8

Sources: Tanzi and Schuknecht (2000),OECD Economic Outlook (June 2016, Annex Table 29), and OECD data bank.

government spending is nearly 40 per cent of national income, higher than in Australia. The 'continental' model is often regarded as being distinct from what is often described as the 'Anglo-Saxon neo-liberal' model, and yet, interestingly, government spending in Germany as a proportion of national income is more or less identical to that in the UK. There certainly are some continental outliers, with the governments of Italy, Sweden, Austria, Belgium and France (the latter shown in this table) all spending over 50 per cent of national income. However, the UK is, in fact, above the OECD average.

Indeed, the figures in Table 1, it can be argued, understate the rise in government spending that has taken place. In the table, national income is measured at market prices. Some regard this as inappropriate given that the market price measure of GDP includes taxes that are levied on goods and services that are sold rather than the underlying costs of those goods and services. If we measure government spending as a proportion of national income measured at what is known as 'factor cost', the current level of government spending is just over 45 per cent of national income. Indeed, using the factor-cost measure of national income, government spending in the UK overtook private spending in the late 2000s, before falling back to its current level of a little less than half of national income.

Government spending, taxation and growth

One of the major objectives of this book is to examine the impact of taxation on growth. However, the focus in much of the data and analysis is on government spending rather than taxation. The reason is that, ultimately, it is government spending that determines the total tax burden. Especially in recent years, government spending has been considerably higher than taxation with the difference being made up by government borrowing. However, government borrowing requires financing and consumes real resources that could have an alternative use. Furthermore, government borrowing leads to a future tax burden. There are potential qualifications to this argument, such as the fact that the debt burden falls (all other things being equal) as nominal national income grows. However, as a rule of thumb, it is assumed in much of this book that it is the financing of government spending that ultimately imposes a burden on the private sector rather than taxation as such. The focus is therefore very much on government spending as the main long-run determinant of the tax burden.

Can government spending be growth enhancing?

Not all government spending harms economic growth. For example, notwithstanding the literature on private governance (see, for example, Stringham 2015), it can be argued that effective judicial and policing systems are necessary for a thriving business economy. Furthermore, it is possible that investment in certain forms of economic activity (such as pure research) has public good qualities and will be under-provided in an entirely free market. Infrastructure such as ports and roads can also be important for promoting economic growth. In all these cases, there are arguments for private provision rather than state provision. But, even if spending on infrastructure or research is not as efficient in the public as in the private sector, such spending could still increase growth as long as the rate of return from the spending is greater than zero.

Despite this, we should be cautious about assuming that even government investment and research spending will lead to higher growth, though it is more likely to do so than other categories of government spending. In Part 2 of this book, Patrick Minford suggests that tax-financed government spending on investment or on research and development reduces economic growth because the negative impact on growth of the taxes levied to finance the spending outweighs any positive impact on growth of the spending itself. This may be because, among other reasons, government-financed investment is determined by political criteria rather than economic criteria and so is not growth enhancing in practice even if it could be in theory.

Economic growth versus other measures of welfare

Government spending could improve economic welfare even if it does not lead to more economic growth as conventionally measured. For example, the provision of welfare benefits to the very poor may reduce growth both because of the effects on incentives of the taxes levied to finance the benefits and also because the welfare benefits themselves might reduce incentives to work and save. However, such welfare benefits might still be regarded as desirable.

There is also a huge range of government and private sector activities the welfare impact of which is imperfectly measured in national income accounts. This is true to such an extent that we may have no real idea whether a particular category of government spending reduces economic welfare to a greater or lesser extent than is indicated by national income figures. Government spending on arts might enrich society in ways that cannot be captured in economic growth figures. However, on the other hand, arts spending might have no welfare benefit whatsoever and be totally wasted and yet it would appear in national income figures at the amount spent rather than at the increase in societal welfare (zero).

When it comes to taxation, a reduction in measured growth arising from reduced work effort caused by the higher taxes necessary to finance higher spending is likely to be compensated in welfare terms at least to some extent by an increase in leisure time. The value of that increase in leisure time would not appear in national income accounts at all, whereas the value of the reduction in working hours would be fully captured as a reduction in growth.

While it is difficult to be precise, taking all these issues into consideration, it is likely to be the case that the point at which government spending and taxation maximise welfare will be beyond the point at which government spending and taxation maximise economic growth.

It is also worth noting that there are some taxes that could, in theory at least, enhance economic welfare and even economic growth. For example, taxes on negative spillover effects from consumption or production activities of businesses might reduce those effects to a level that is more socially optimal. Designing such taxes though is difficult in practice and often their levels will be determined by political rather than economic considerations. However, in principle, such taxes could raise economic welfare while replacing other taxes that are more harmful.

The revenue-maximising level of government spending

Although governments do not necessarily act rationally and practical government decisions can be determined by a whole range of factors such as the actions of vested interests, in principle at least, it would seem sensible for governments to spend money on functions that both enhanced growth or other aspects of economic welfare. At some point, however, the ability of the government to find spending projects that will enhance growth will be exhausted. Furthermore, the effect on growth of the taxes necessary to finance spending is likely to increase with the level of tax.

Eventually, the impact of additional taxes on growth may be so large that the fall in growth caused by raising taxes will actually lead to a drop in tax revenues. In other words, attempts to raise taxes further will actually reduce tax revenue and consequently lead to a reduction rather than an increase in government spending. The higher marginal rates of tax will generate no net revenue because of the shrinkage of the tax base caused by the extra taxes. This shrinkage of the tax base can be caused by lower growth, higher levels of illegal tax evasion or by legal tax avoidance. The point at which taxes cannot be raised further without reducing revenues is often described as the top of the Laffer curve.

If it follows that there is a point beyond which further increases in tax rates can reduce tax revenues, it also follows that some governments might spend at such high levels that it is possible for them to reduce tax rates and actually increase revenues. In other words, in some high tax countries, it might be possible to reduce the burden of taxation and increase government spending. Even if that is not true in aggregate it might be true with regard to particular taxes. For example, it might be possible that reducing inheritance tax or the highest rate of income tax will increase tax yields even if there are other taxes which could generate increased revenue if they were increased.

When the UK government reduced the 50 per cent top tax rate, for example, it conducted a serious analysis of the dynamic behavioural effects.[1] Her Majesty's Revenue and Customs (HMRC) identified a number of potential impacts on behaviour. Their analysis suggested that, if there was no effect on economic behaviour,

---

1   http://webarchive.nationalarchives.gov.uk/20140109143644/http:/www.hmrc.gov
    .uk/budget2012/excheq-income-tax-2042.pdf

the Treasury would lose around £3.5 billion as a result of reducing the top tax rate from 50 per cent to 45 per cent. However, as a result of behavioural effects (identified to include, among other factors, reduced hours worked; reduced foreign direct investment; greater avoidance, tax planning and evasion; and reduced human capital formation) any decrease in tax revenue would be more or less totally reversed, making the revenue impact of the reduction in the top rate of tax negligible.

In practice, there would appear to have been a number of historical examples of governments reducing tax rates and seeing large increases in revenue. For example, as explained by Laffer (2012), in 1978 the US brought in the Steiger–Hansen capital gains tax rate reduction and then, during the following 25 years or so, there were larger cuts in taxes. The results were interesting. In 1980, the top 1 per cent of income earners paid taxes equal to 1.5 per cent of GDP or 17.5 per cent of all the income taxes in the US. By 2007, the top 1 per cent of income earners paid 3.2 per cent of GDP in income taxes and they paid 42.5 per cent of all the income taxes collected. There was a very similar trend in the UK after Nigel Lawson's reduction in the top rates of tax in 1988.

Where does the UK stand?

The above analysis suggests that there are three points we can identify when looking at the appropriate level of government spending and taxation. The first point we hit is the growth-maximising level of government spending as a proportion of national income. Secondly, there is the welfare-maximising level of government spending. Thirdly, there is the maximum level of government spending beyond which any attempt to raise taxes will actually lead to lower tax revenues. In Chapter 5, David Smith suggests that the growth-maximising share of government spending in GDP is probably in the range 18.5–23.5 per cent of national income, using current (July 2016) UK definitions at market prices. The welfare-maximising share is probably in the range 26.5–32.5 per cent of national income. The maximum sustainable level of government spending is probably in the range 37–38 per cent of national income.[2]

Of course, there is a great deal of uncertainty attached to these numbers, even with the ranges suggested. In practice, the welfare-maximising level of taxation and government spending will depend on the institutional environment in which the private sector can provide welfare, infrastructure and so on. These levels will also depend on the shape of the tax system and how government spending is allocated. If we have a badly designed tax system and government spending determined to a greater degree by vested interests and rent seekers, the optimal level of government spending is likely to be lower. However, what is perhaps most alarming is that, even on the projections set out in the March 2016 Budget and without any relaxation of the purse strings by the new administration, government spending will only just come down to sustainable levels by 2020/21.

Recent trends in types of government spending

While there was a dramatic increase in government spending in the last century, it is also of note that, as government spending has grown, it has become more focused on areas that tend to harm growth more or help growth less. For example, government spending on investment has fallen from over 6 per cent of national income in the late 1960s to less than 3 per cent today. Also since the late 1960s, welfare payments have almost doubled as a percentage of national income to their current levels of around 14 per cent (this excludes health and education spending).

---

2 This is slightly different conceptually from the top of the Laffer curve, but both concepts would give rise to similar empirical results.

In the period from 2010–15, there has been further significant reorientation of spending. Public order and safety (comprising major parts of the 'nightwatchman' functions of the state) had reductions in real spending of about 15 per cent. Meanwhile, spending on both health and social protection increased in real terms. There is no sign of these trends being reversed. Indeed, they are likely to continue in the years to 2020.

Regional differences

Although government spending is around 45 per cent of national income in the country as a whole, there are considerable regional variations. Some government spending in high-spending regions is financed by transfers from low-spending regions. The high-spending regions do not therefore bear all the costs in terms of reduced growth of the taxes necessary to finance their spending. However, insofar as spending is directed towards programmes that reduce work incentives and crowd out private sector activity, there may still be a reduction in growth in those regions with high levels of government spending.

When looking at growth and government spending across the regions it is, of course, difficult to work out cause and effect – do the regions have low growth because they have high levels of government spending or does the government finance high levels of transfers to certain regions because they have experienced low growth? Nevertheless, the figures shown in Table 2, which is a summary of Table 10, are dramatic. Table 2 shows government spending as a proportion of local gross value added for one high-spending, one low-spending and one average-spending region of the UK, together with data on workless households and gross value added per head in the economy.

Perhaps the most interesting observation is the fact that, if London were a country, it would have among the lowest government spending ratios in the OECD. Secondly, the spending ratios

Table 2   UK general government expenditure in 2012/13 – regional data

	Ratio of government spending to GDP at basic prices (%)	Public sector employment in 2016 Q1 (%)	Workless households in 2014 (%)	GVA per head in 2014 (£)
North East	69.7	20.3	21.7	18,216
Eastern England	46.0	15.3	12.7	23,063
London	30.1	14.3	14.6	42,666
Wales	74.3	21.3	19.4	17,573
Northern Ireland	76.5	25.3	21.4	18,682
UK	48.2	17.0	16.4	24,616

Source: HM Treasury *Public Expenditure Statistical Analysis 2014*, 1 August 2015, Office for National Statistics *Regional Gross Value Added (Income Approach), 1997 to 2014*, 9 December 2015, *Public Employment Statistical Bulletin*, 15 June 2016 and *Workless Households for Regions across the UK*, 6 October 2015. A workless household contains at least one person aged 16–64 where no one aged 16 or over is in employment.

in the North East, Northern Ireland and Wales are beyond anything that is seen in developed countries.

But what about austerity?

The coalition government came to office in 2010 with an agenda to control government borrowing. This involved significant tax increases, but also proposed spending cuts. In public discourse around the so-called austerity agenda, some dramatic figures were often bandied around. There are two reasons for that. The first is that spending cuts were often defined relative to previous projected increases in spending. The second reason is that many government functions were protected from cuts while some functions were cut more deeply, as has been noted above.

So, what has the record been overall? Between 2010 and 2015, total government spending actually increased by 4.6 per cent. In real terms, government spending fell by just 0.5 per cent a year.

Real spending per capita fell by a little more – by about 1 per cent per year. In other words, the overall adjustment in government spending was very small indeed – certainly, many private sector households and businesses had to make much greater adjustments to their budgets given the economic realities that they faced after the financial crash. The large government spending cuts often quoted in the media relate not to the overall government spending settlement but to the strategic choices that the last two governments have made to focus more spending on foreign aid, the health service, schools and social protection spending for older people.

It is important in debates about government spending to make this distinction. It is reasonable to debate whether the overall level of spending is too high or too low. At the same time, we can have a separate debate about spending priorities within the overall spending envelope. Overall, as has been noted above, government spending remained at over 45 per cent of national income (at factor cost) by the end of the coalition government.

Over the next few years, if anything, the picture is projected to be even less austere. Through to 2020, nominal government spending is planned to continue to rise, real government spending to go up slightly and spending as a proportion of national income at factor cost to fall to 41 per cent. In other words, government spending will only fall relative to national income and not in absolute or real terms.

Why does taxation affect economic growth?

For reasons already discussed, it is possible that the impact of taxation on underlying economic welfare may be different from its effect on growth. For example, if the government decides to tax the population to provide them with goods and services they would have not chosen to buy, economic welfare will be reduced, but measured growth is unlikely to change. This is because it is

---

Box 1 Key facts – government spending 2010–2020

- Nominal spending rose by 4.6 per cent from 2010 to 2015.
- Real spending fell by 0.5 per cent per annum from 2010 to 2015.
- Real spending per capita fell by 1 per cent per annum from 2010 to 2015.
- Government spending as a proportion of national income measured at factor cost was 45 per cent in 2015.
- Real government spending is planned to rise from 2016 to 2020.
- Government spending on health and social protection rose in real terms from 2010 to 2015.
- Government spending on public order and safety fell in real terms by 15 per cent from 2010 to 2015.
- By 2020, government spending as a proportion of national income measured at factor cost is planned to be over 40 per cent – this is before any relaxation of the purse strings as hinted by the new government.

normally the amount the government spends on the provision of services that enters national income computations in the absence of any measure of 'market value'. Furthermore, very often government will provide services less efficiently than the private sector could provide them. (See, for example, Niemietz (2016) and the references contained therein.) However, national income measurement systems rarely take this into account.

At the same time, as discussed above, some forms of government expenditure will be welfare and/or growth enhancing. For example, if a country needs to be defended from external threats or if it is necessary to have a government-funded police force, a court system and government-funded infrastructure, the provision of such services might well enhance growth (by providing a better environment for the business sector). Furthermore, such services might actually have a higher value than the amount of money spent on them by government.[3]

However, it is inconceivable that the government will tax its citizens and provide government-funded services to the right level and in the right areas. Public choice economics (see, for example, Tullock et al. 2002) suggests that goods and services will be provided beyond the optimal level and that governments will also not provide goods, services and income transfers in a way that maximises welfare. Instead, they will respond to pressure from interest groups who might act as voters, lobbyists or government employees in order to redirect government spending towards their favoured projects. Indeed, the particular spending priorities of the current government, as discussed above, were predicted and analysed by Booth (2008) and Willetts (2011).

Notwithstanding the above comments, taxation and government spending will also affect measured national income and economic growth. They do this in a variety of ways which can be summarised as follows:

- Taxation can lead to reduced incentives to supply labour and save and invest if wages and the returns to saving and investment are taxed heavily.
- Taxation on businesses and personal investment income and capital gains can reduce the incentive to innovate and take entrepreneurial risks.
- Discriminatory taxes in relation to different goods and services can lead to what economists call 'deadweight losses'. Such discriminatory taxes lead people to buy products that

---

3 It is worth noting again that there is a great deal of debate about the extent to which such services and infrastructure need to be provided by the government, as opposed to the private, sector.

they value less rather than products they value more purely for tax reasons.[4]

- Specific taxes such as stamp duty charged only on transactions discourage people from moving house or exchanging assets in other ways.
- Tax-financed welfare benefits can reduce work incentives, incentives to train or take promotion, and incentives to save.

As should be clear from the above discussion, it is not a foregone conclusion that all increases in taxes at all times will have a negative impact on growth. The extent of the impact of tax on economic growth will depend on how responsive entrepreneurs, workers and savers are to the changes in net profits, wages and interest that result from the imposition of taxes and on other factors discussed above. So, ultimately, the question has to be investigated empirically. What does the empirical evidence say?

Tax and growth: the evidence

The main approach economists have used to investigate the impact of tax on growth is through the development of what are known as 'growth regressions'. Sophisticated data sets are used to estimate the effect of a range of economic variables on economic growth, including taxation and government spending.

The results of these growth regressions are clear. Taxation has a strong relationship with growth – the higher the level of taxation and government spending, the lower the level of growth. Not only that, the effect is significant and substantial. There is a summary of all the main studies in Part 2. However, the headline result is easy to summarise. As a rough estimate, a rise of

---

4   The most obvious example here is value added tax, which is not charged at the full rate on all goods and services in the UK. This includes, for example, domestic fuel. The government has a range of schemes that try to reduce carbon emissions, but the tax system strongly encourages domestic fuel consumption.

10 percentage points in the ratio of taxation to national income reduces growth by 0.5–1.0 per cent per annum. Indeed, an OECD study has suggested that up to one third of the growth deceleration in the OECD between 1965 and 1995 could be explained by higher taxes. Furthermore, because in some European countries tax burdens have increased much more dramatically than the OECD average it is likely that there would have been correspondingly larger effects on their growth rates (Leibfritz et al. 1997).

Despite the apparent consensus in the growth–regression literature, economists do not necessarily find it convincing in terms of identifying a causal relationship between tax and growth. The very strong association found in such work does not demonstrate causality and certainly does not do so in particular situations. For example, an apparent relationship between growth and lower taxation might arise as a result of a third factor which affects both (such as good legal institutions and the rule of law). The regressions might also be affected by outliers or particular circumstances that pertained at particular times or in specific groups of countries.

It may well be implausible, given the very high level of government spending in Western countries and given the consistent results of the growth regression literature, that a reduction in government spending and taxation would not increase growth – and substantially so. However, the growth regression literature does not prove that.

Given these doubts, more robust examination and modelling of the data was commissioned for this study and undertaken by Lucy Minford. The results of this are also reported in Part 2. Minford uses modelling techniques that are particularly robust and which are very powerful at rejecting false models. There are two other insights which also make her work interesting.

Tax rates often have their impact at the margin. It is the additional tax that an individual will pay on additional earnings that will determine their desire to work, save or take business

---

Box 2   Dynamic scoring[1]

An important practical and policy reason for examining the relationship between tax and growth is given by the UK government's recent exercises in so-called dynamic scoring (HMRC 2013, 2014). These papers represent the first efforts of a UK government to model the dynamic macroeconomic impacts of proposed tax reforms using what is known as a calibrated computable general equilibrium (CGE) model. CGE models of this type are used by the US Congressional Budget Office to analyse the effects of tax cuts. The UK corporation tax exercise (HMRC 2013) is based on the premise that, while reducing corporation tax rates represents a static cost to the Exchequer in lost revenues, it implies dynamic gains through the stimulation of business investment via the reduction in the cost of capital, and transitional productivity growth which, by raising taxable profits, allow much of that cost to be recovered.

If dynamic scoring is not used to assess the impact of tax changes, the government might overestimate the cost to the Exchequer of tax reductions or overestimate the revenue to be gained from tax increases. This could lead to serious policy misjudgements.

---

1   The substance and technical detail of this box follow very closely Minford (2015). However, the conclusions have been adapted by the author of the introduction to relate it to the discussion in the rest of this book.

risks. Lucy Minford therefore uses the top marginal tax rate in her analysis of the effect of tax on growth. Secondly, regulation is often used as a substitute for taxation to achieve similar objectives. One obvious example of this is the minimum wage, which

The approach exemplifies the stance of the coalition government elected in 2010 and its successor Conservative government elected in 2015, that growth is a key policy objective: corporation tax reductions have been central to the government's drive to stimulate growth and investment through supply side reforms (HMRC 2013: 5).

It is not uncontroversial. Adam and Bozio (2009: 20), for example, point out that 'dynamic scoring requires making numerous modelling assumptions and essentially guessing the parameters *for which no hard empirical evidence is available*. This opens the door to large controversies if these guesses are made – or perceived to be made – in a politically biased way' (my italics). They go on to say:

Proponents of tax cuts often argue that the economic effects are large. As noted earlier, health and safety regulations might be costly for businesses to implement, reducing profits, employment and tax revenue; or they might lead to a healthier and more productive workforce, with the opposite result. The nature and magnitude of these effects is likely to be exactly what proponents and opponents of regulations dispute. A body responsible for dynamic scoring is in effect asked to pass judgement.

is designed to increase the incomes of the poor so that there is less reliance on benefits financed by taxation.

Lucy Minford constructs a measure that combines both tax and regulatory factors into one index and examines how changes from the trend in that index affect growth. Overall, very strong evidence is found from this study that taxation affects growth, most likely through the channel of reduced entrepreneurship.

Of course, sensitivity tests can be conducted around important parameters, but this amounts to an admission that the range of potential effects could be extremely large.

The issue of dynamic scoring is therefore difficult. Lower taxes may well have a beneficial effect on growth, though the magnitude of that effect is widely disputed. On the other hand, if the government does not use dynamic scoring, it implicitly assumes that the impact of changes in taxes on variables such as economic growth and entrepreneurship is zero.

It is important to note that, when dynamic scoring is used, the government is examining the impacts of particular tax changes rather than the impact of changing the total tax burden. One of the purposes of the further modelling undertaken later in this book is to shed more light on the relationship between tax and growth. However, as far as the state of knowledge that currently exists within the Treasury is concerned, dynamic scoring is probably best used to give an indication of the potential range of effects arising from tax changes. Otherwise, there is a real danger of spurious accuracy.

The research finds that a 10 percentage point fall in a combined index of the top marginal tax rate and regulation relative to its trend produces a rise in output over about thirty years of 24 per cent. This is equivalent to an increase in the growth rate over the thirty years following the cut of about 0.8 percentage points per annum. The model does not distinguish between regulation and tax. However, it is changes in marginal tax rates that have driven the changes in the combined index over the period. As such, it is reasonable to infer that a 10 percentage point cut in the top marginal tax rate would bring about the improvement in growth indicated by the model. Given the government's own research about the dynamic impact of reducing the top rate of tax from 50 per cent to 45 per cent, this result is hardly a surprise.

Designing an effective tax system

Principles of an effective tax system

Though much of this book is about the impact of taxation and government spending on growth in general, the detail of the tax system is also important for economic performance. A badly designed tax system could, all other things equal, have a much greater cost in terms of economic growth and welfare.

The methods by which governments raise taxes can affect economic growth through several channels. For example, taxes can be designed in ways that make them expensive for taxpayers to pay. This may raise the cost of establishing a business (especially as the costs of tax collection tend to be a fixed cost and therefore bear especially heavily on small businesses). More generally, unnecessary costs of tax collection are a deadweight cost on the economy. In addition, if there is uncertainty in the tax system, this can reduce the incentives for individuals and businesses to invest as it raises the risk premium required for investment. Thirdly, taxes can be costly if they discriminate against particular economic activities. This can distort decision making and lead individuals and businesses to take decisions that reduce welfare. This arises because the relative tax treatment of two courses of action can lead the less valuable one to appear more remunerative after tax is taken into account.

There are two exceptions to these general rules. Firstly, higher taxes on activities that have what economists call negative externalities (that is, social costs or negative spillover effects on the rest of the economy) can increase welfare if they are well designed and targeted. That is because the taxes reflect the additional costs to society of such activities that are not reflected in market prices. Secondly, mobile factors of production should be relatively lightly taxed because their behaviour is affected by taxes to a greater extent than that of factors of production that are not mobile. This would justify lower taxes on capital or on labour that was especially mobile.[5] Conversely, factors of production that are extremely inelastic in terms of their supply can be more heavily taxed without affecting economic growth, the obvious example here being undeveloped land.

A new tax system for the UK

Overall, Rory Meakin, the author of Part 3 of this book, proposes the abolition of twenty taxes which are especially badly designed. These include inheritance tax and also some comparatively new taxes such as the apprenticeship levy. It is proposed that other taxes should be radically reformed too in order to create a coherent tax system designed to raise 20–25 per cent of national income.

Such a system would include the following major taxes:

- An income tax set at a rate of 15 per cent of income above a personal allowance of around £10,000.
- A value added tax (VAT) of 12.5 per cent, with most reduced-rate, zero-rated and exempt items charged tax at this standard rate.
- A new housing consumption tax on rents and imputed rents designed to mimic VAT at 12.5 per cent.
- A new land value tax.
- A much-reduced fuel duty.

The move away from existing property taxes and towards a land value tax and a tax on the imputed rent from owner-occupied

---

5   For example, this would justify a special system of taxes applying to 'non-doms' (those who are not permanently resident), as already exists in the UK.

housing (or a housing consumption tax) would create a tax system much more conducive to growth. Existing taxes on business property would be abolished and homeowners would no longer suffer stamp duty when they moved to take a more productive job. The tax on imputed rent would end the bias against rented property that exists in the UK tax system and a land value tax is well understood by economists to be one of the least growth-inhibiting taxes available.

Instead of separate taxes on corporate profits, income from shares would be taxed in a similar way as income from corporate bonds,[6] thus ending the tax incentive companies currently have to take on more debt.

This set of taxes would be much easier to administer than the current UK tax code, which is among the most complex in the developed world. There would be a small number of taxes levied at low rates with no exemptions.

It is often thought that reducing taxes and making taxes 'flatter' tend to help the rich and harm the poor. That is not the case with the proposed reform. Currently, the less-well-off pay a high proportion of their income in 'sin' taxes levied on products the governments deems to be harmful such as alcohol. The reduction in those taxes and other aspects of the package (the proposed property taxes, for example, are likely to affect the better off to a greater degree) mean that, overall, lower income deciles gain from the proposed tax reform. The modelling undertaken by Rory Meakin suggests that the poorest decile would enjoy tax cuts worth 26 per cent of gross income, followed by 19 per cent for the second poorest decile, 17 per cent for the third poorest decile and then 13 per cent for the fourth poorest decile. The third richest decile would enjoy a cut of just 9 per cent while the richest two deciles would both see their taxes cut by 13 per cent of their incomes.

---

6   That is, in the hands of the investor.

As well as changes to the tax system, a number of changes to the way in which taxes are administered are proposed in Part 3. These would make the tax system much more stable, predictable and less prone to short-term political meddling.

Conclusion

Overall, the authors of this important study make a major contribution to the understanding of the role of taxation in a modern state. The extent to which the size of government has increased would probably take many by surprise. Furthermore, the extent of so-called austerity has been limited and will continue to be so. What has happened is that the government has made strategic choices to increase government spending in some areas and to reduce it in others.

Politicians who purport to govern in the name of promoting the welfare of all should be aware that taxation and government spending are not only beyond the levels at which economic growth would be maximised but almost certainly way above the levels which would be most beneficial for economic welfare. More worryingly, it is quite possible that, in the UK, government spending is at or beyond maximum sustainable levels. Certainly, there would be significant benefits to economic growth from reducing government spending and taxation, which would ultimately benefit all sections of society.

If the UK had a more coherent tax system, the same amount of revenue could be raised at a much lower economic cost. Such a tax system would involve the elimination of huge numbers of taxes and the simplification of many others. The UK has had successive Chancellors of the Exchequers who have systematically sought to make the tax system more complex for political purposes at great economic cost. There is now an opportunity to reverse the damage. However, it will be much easier to do so at lower levels of government spending and taxation.

References

Adam, S. and Bozio, A. (2009) Dynamic scoring. *OECD Journal on Budgeting* 9(2): 99–124.

Booth, P. M. (2008) The impossibility of progress – a public choice analysis of state pension provision. In *Pension Provision: Government Failure Around the World* (ed. P. Booth, O. Juurikkala and N. Silver), Readings 63, pp. 95–125. London: Institute of Economic Affairs.

HMRC (2013) Analysis of the dynamic effects of corporation tax reductions. HM Revenue and Customs, HM Treasury (www.gov.uk/government/publications).

HMRC (2014) Analysis of the dynamic effects of fuel duty reductions. HM Revenue and Customs, HM Treasury (www.gov.uk/government/publications).

Laffer, A. (2012) *The Laffer Curve and the Failure of Stimulus Spending.* Current Controversies 38. London: Institute of Economic Affairs.

Leibfritz, W., Thornton, J. and Bibbee, A. (1997) Taxation and economic performance. OECD Economics Department Working Papers 176. Paris: OECD.

Minford, L. (2015) The macroeconomic effects of UK tax, regulation and R&D subsidies: testing endogenous growth hypotheses in an open economy DSGE model. PhD thesis, Cardiff University.

Niemietz, K. (2016) Is the NHS underfunded? *EA Magazine* (Spring), pp. 7–10.

Stringham, E. P. (2015) *Private Governance: Creating Order in Economic and Social Life.* Oxford University Press.

Tanzi, V. and Schuknecht, L. (2000) *Public Spending in the 20th Century: A Global Perspective.* Cambridge University Press.

Tullock, G., Brady, G. L. and Seldon, A. (2002) *Government Failure: A Primer in Public Choice.* Washington, DC: Cato Institute.

Willetts, D. (2011) *The Pinch: How the Baby Boomers Took Their Children's Future – And Why They Should Give It Back.* London: Atlantic Books.

PART 1

THE GROWTH OF GOVERNMENT 1870–2020

2 HOW SHOULD GOVERNMENT SPENDING AND TAX BURDENS BE MEASURED?

David B. Smith

Introduction

The main theme of this chapter is the practical problems that arise when trying to measure the burdens of government spending and taxation and how these have developed since the late nineteenth century, both internationally and in Britain. All systems of measurement, such as the National Accounts figures compiled by the UK Office for National Statistics (ONS), are based on some underlying conceptual framework, even if this might be implicit or lost in the mists of time. For example, the statistics for gross domestic product (GDP) that appear in the national accounts were originally built around a Keynesian 'effective demand' paradigm in order to help maximise British military production in World War II. As a result, the GDP data are not necessarily well suited for other purposes, including trying to differentiate between government and private-sector activities.

Because it is important to be clear about the conceptual underpinnings from the start, this chapter commences with two simple truisms that tend to be largely forgotten in the political debate on 'tax and spend' issues. The first truism is that the government has effectively zero resources of its own. The corollary is that, under normal circumstances, all government spending commitments imply higher taxes, either immediately or in the future, when the increased debt resulting from borrowing has to be serviced.[1] The second truism, which follows on from the first, is that the tax base is not total GDP, as appears to be believed by politicians and officials, but only the residual component of GDP after government spending has been subtracted.[2] This is because it is impossible for any institution (or individual) to generate resources through taxing itself. In logic, real resources always have to come from outside the boundaries of the body concerned. Each of these two truisms will be considered in turn.

It is government spending and not taxation that determines the burden of government activity

In the distant past, monarchs had revenues from their own private lands, which were known as the 'Royal Domain' and most of today's Western governments enjoy non-tax receipts of some 2 per cent to 3½ per cent of GDP from sources such as rent, interest and dividend payments. However, the share of government spending in GDP currently runs from just over one third to something over one half in developed countries (Table 7), implying that all additional government spending eventually requires

---

1 The fact that all government expenditure has to be paid for has been known since the 1960s as the 'government's budget constraint'. There is a third option, borrowing from the banking sector. However, this is only non-inflationary during the temporary period that lending to the private sector is being crowded off the asset side of bank balance sheets. Once nearly all bank lending is to the government, any extra loans to the public sector boost bank liabilities – i.e. their deposits – and hence broad money. This is the 'monetisation' point at which inflation (and, in extreme cases, hyper-inflation) starts to take off.

2 For convenience, this will be referred to as private-sector (or 'non-socialised') GDP from now on. However, this is something of a misnomer because, being a residual item, public corporations and non-profit-making institutions are also included. The measurement problems involved are discussed more fully later. The term 'market sector' might also be applied to that part of GDP which theoretically responds to market signals rather than being determined by bureaucrats and politicians. However, the Office for National Statistics uses the term 'Market Sector Gross Value Added' to denote a rather different volume series in the national accounts. It was decided that it might cause confusion to employ the same terminology here.

Figure 1 Ratio of UK non-oil tax receipts to UK non-oil GDP at factor cost 1900–2015

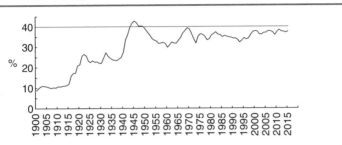

higher taxes under 'normal circumstances'. These can be defined as a situation in which the economy concerned is: (1) running at reasonably full employment, and (2) not taxing to such an extent that a reduction in tax rates will generate more tax revenue. These are important qualifications, however, and have been hotly debated for decades.

Figure 1 shows the ratio of taxes to UK GDP since 1900. It suggests that the upper limit on taxable capacity is somewhat below 40 per cent of the factor-cost measure of GDP; the average figure during the twenty-first century has been 37.3 per cent, for example. However, as will be discussed below, this is only one possible measure of the tax burden.

Keynesian economists have long argued that in circumstances of mass unemployment small increases in government spending can induce a significantly larger increase in GDP; the ratio between the two being the Keynesian 'multiplier'. However, most empirical estimates suggest that the multiplier can be negative as well as positive and is probably not much higher than one or two at most. Since government spending is included in the definition of GDP, the multiplier has to be greater than one before there is any improvement in private-sector activity as a result of increased government spending. Otherwise, increased public expenditure simply crowds out private activity, and exacerbates the contraction in the latter, and this may have been what has happened internationally since the global financial crash. Unfortunately, the literature dealing with the multiplier has sometimes fallen into the trap of reducing complex systems of multivariate relationships to a simple ratio. The value of the multiplier is conditional on all the other variables in the system – including the reactions of the monetary authorities – and should not be expected to be stable over time, except by extreme coincidence.

The Laffer curve argument cuts the other way, of course, and suggests that beyond a certain point tax-financed increases in government spending lead to a reduction in aggregate supply, which is assumed to be fixed in simple Keynesian models.[3] The introduction of a flexible supply side, which is influenced by the post-tax incentives to produce goods and services, noticeably alters the conclusions from conventional analyses that assume aggregate supply is fixed (see Smith 2006; Sinclair 2012). One important conclusion is that the long-term negative supply-side effects of the higher taxes associated with budget deficits have to be traded off against any short-term demand stimulus from increased spending. This point appears to have been rather forgotten since the financial crash of 2008.

Because the supply-side approach was heavily rooted in the 'public finance' literature, which tended to assume that all government spending was tax financed, it was originally left slightly vague as to whether tax-financed spending was more, or less, harmful than the deficit-financed sort, or whether both were equivalent in the long run. If deficit-financed spending is

---

3   It remains something of a mystery why supply shocks have not been given more prominence in the macroeconomic debate. Almost a quarter of a century ago, Sterne and Bayoumi (1993) used time series methods to examine whether it was demand or supply shocks that produced the greatest disturbances to growth and inflation in the case of 21 OECD countries. They concluded that both effects were roughly equally important in the short term but that supply shocks dominated in the medium term in the ratio 72:28 where output was concerned.

as harmful as tax-financed spending, then the relevant macro-economic concern becomes the public spending burden and not the tax burden. How government spending is financed becomes a secondary issue.

The Ricardian Equivalence theorem (Barro 1974) argued that any alleged stimulatory effects from deficit-financed public expenditure were likely to prove minimal if people rationally feared higher future taxes, as a result of running a budget deficit today and therefore reduced their consumption or investment. In such circumstances, the macroeconomic consequences of taxation and spending become identical in the long run.[4] While full Ricardian Equivalence remains controversial, it certainly seems to exist to some extent – i.e. it is not zero – but it may be less than 100 per cent.

In addition to Ricardian Equivalence effects, private capital formation also seems to be reduced by budget deficits, because of the uncertainties created with regard to future taxes and interest rates. This suggests that when spending is financed by deficits it will ultimately crowd out roughly the same volume of activity as if it is financed by taxes – though the effects of financing spending via taxes might come through less quickly. Indeed, in this context, it is conceivable that the present sluggish growth observable in so many Western economies reflects the supply-side hangover that followed the Keynesian-inspired public spending binge that was the politicians' reaction to the financial crash.

This analysis suggests that the tax burden ought really to be measured by looking at total government spending which is financed by taxes and borrowing (in effect, deferred taxes in most cases). The ratio of general government expenditure to national income is shown in Figure 2.

---

4   This does not invalidate the insights from the public finance approach indicating that high marginal rates of tax, and regulatory induced distortions, can both do severe microeconomic damage and lead to a reduction in aggregate supply that then has macroeconomic implications.

No institution can tax itself

The second important truism, which follows from the previous analysis, is that the tax base is not total gross domestic product (GDP) but only the residual component of GDP after government spending has been subtracted – in other words, we should focus on the burden of government on the private sector. Individual arms of government pay taxes to other parts of government (e.g. local authorities pay VAT on their purchases). However, these transfers net out for government as a whole, even if this is not always apparent in the published statistics.

Regrettably, the longer-term projections for tax receipts made by the Office for Budget Responsibility (OBR) appear to be largely driven by their predictions for money GDP. However, the public/private distinction is highly important when forecasting because the ratio of private to total GDP shows marked cyclical swings (see Figure 2). Some of the forecasting errors in the official predictions of government receipts from the OBR – and HM Treasury before them[5] – may have resulted from a failure to distinguish between the public and private sector components of GDP. However, making this distinction in practice is not entirely straightforward, as will be seen shortly.

Because there are limits to an economy's taxable capacity, and increasing the share of national output absorbed by the state can reduce output per head and crowd out future growth,[6] it is essential to have accurate measures of public spending and tax burdens. Furthermore, it is important that these measures are defined consistently over time. This is both for politically important monitoring purposes – for example, to see whether

---

5   The OBR is still working with the former HM Treasury forecasting model and many OBR staff are former Treasury employees.

6   See Sinclair (2012: 82–84) for a tabular summary of the published studies in this area from 1975 onwards.

Figure 2   Ratios of UK general government expenditure and private
expenditure to UK GDP at factor cost 1870–2015

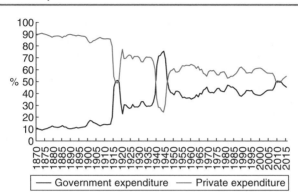

the government has abided by its spending plans[7] – and to allow politically disinterested research to be undertaken into the wider consequences of government spending, borrowing and taxes. Unfortunately, the devil lies in the detail where measurement is concerned. This is partly because defining the boundary between the public and private sectors is often surprisingly difficult.

Measurement difficulties are exacerbated by the fact that official statisticians frequently rework their figures onto new – and, often, surprisingly incompatible – conceptual bases. One example is the European Union (EU) mandated switch from the 1995 European Standard Accounts (ESA 1995) to the new ESA 2010 national accounts conventions in the autumn of 2014.[8] This switchover led to extremely large methodological changes

---

7   It will be seen later that there have been so many definitional changes since Mr Osborne introduced his first Budget after the 2010 election that it is almost impossible to know how far he succeeded or failed to achieve his fiscal goals during his six years as Chancellor. It is because Parliament's control of the purse is the foundation stone of British democracy that this has serious constitutional implications.

8   These figures are used to determine fiscal transfers between the EU member states and correspondingly have a quasi-legal status.

Figure 3   Ratio of UK general government expenditure to private GDP and non-oil taxes to non-oil private GDP 1900–2015

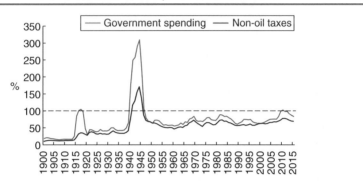

to the published figures for both the government accounts and national output, as will be described later. These changes, which were particularly marked in the British case, noticeably reduced the alleged UK tax and spending burdens and led to a retrospective payment to the EU. This is despite the fact that nothing can have changed in reality because the past is past.

Once it has been agreed how to measure national income, in theory, measuring the sizes of the government and private sectors might appear to be a simple matter. Conceptually, all that is required is agreed measures of national output and government spending. 'Private' (or 'non-socialised') spending can then be calculated as a residual item. Calculating the ratios of government spending and taxes to private GDP then becomes straightforward if it is thought that this is the best measure of the burden that the state is imposing on society (Figure 3). In practice, however, disturbingly incompatible estimates of the spending and tax burdens are calculable depending on (1) the exact definitions employed and (2) the particular generation of official data used. Generally, there are two main reasons why competing measures of the public spending and tax burdens differ from each other in any given generation of official data. Each will be considered in turn.

How do we define the public sector?

The first reason is that definitions of the public sector can vary widely, particularly once allowance is made for quasi-government bodies and public corporations, such as the former nationalised industries, universities and the BBC. Since October 2008, such bodies have included the bailed-out banks, such as Lloyds/ HBOS, now being gradually returned to the private sector.[9] More recently, housing associations were incorporated in the public sector figures in February 2016. Bringing housing associations into the definition of public corporations raised estimated public borrowing in 2014/15 by £3.6bn and added £59.8bn to the public sector debt stock.

The convention used by the Organisation of Economic Co-operation and Development (OECD) and similar international bodies to ameliorate this 'fuzzy-boundary' problem is to employ the concept of 'general government'. General government consists of central government and local authorities[10] but excludes public corporations, such as the old nationalised industries, the bailed-out banks and housing associations.

While the exclusion of public corporations is probably inevitable, if reasonably consistent definitions are to be maintained over time, it means that there is probably a downwards bias in some of the figures quoted later. However, any subsidies to loss-making public corporations are included in total general government expenditure. Arguably, public corporations that live off their own resources, and do not receive government financial assistance, are not a direct burden on the taxpayer, while profit-making ones permit lower taxes or more spending than would have been possible otherwise. The main concern then

---

9   The ONS publishes figures both cum and ex these financial institutions. Most people, including the OBR, prefer the figures excluding the state-owned banks and these are the figures used throughout this contribution.

10   And provinces, states, etc., in federal systems.

becomes whether public corporations are efficient producers or whether, instead, they abuse their state-granted monopoly and overcharge customers. In which case, this overcharge has the properties of a covert indirect tax.[11]

Another potential source of downwards bias is that estimates of the tax and spending burdens provide no understanding of the regulatory costs that are increasingly imposed on private economic agents. Such regulations often appear to favour political goals and vested interests rather than society as a whole and can be used as a substitute for taxes.[12] Tanzi (2008) has suggested that one reason for increasing regulation has been that many Western states have run out of spare taxable resources. As a result, politicians have rewarded their client interest groups through regulations, which impose concealed losses on other citizens, because they cannot overtly expropriate any more from the taxpayer. This may reflect growing political resistance in addition to the economic limits on taxable capacity. Nevertheless, these chapters do not examine the burden of regulation.

While accepting that any chosen figure to represent public expenditure has its drawbacks, it was argued in Smith (2006) that the 'least-bad' buys for practical purposes are: (1) to employ the OECD's statistics for international comparisons, and (2) to use the UK Office for National Statistics (ONS) measures of general government expenditure compiled by subsector and economic categories for Britain.

---

11 Paying for the 'green agenda' by means of increased electricity bills is an example. Another grey area is the issue of third-sector organisations that are essentially commissioned by government to deliver public/social services. These make up the bulk of the 'Non-profit institutions serving households' in the expenditure GDP figures in Table 5 and their funding appears in 'Other current grants' in Table 3. The latter have been aggregated with 'Government final current expenditure' in Table 9 to maintain historical consistency.

12 Mr Osborne's imposition of the living wage is a possible example. In theory, it may prevent the bottom end of the labour market clearing – with potential adverse consequences for the employment of less productive employees – but helps reduce government payments to the low paid.

The latter are presented in Table 3 for the latest full fiscal year.[13]

How do we define national output?

The second major problem when measuring the government spending and tax burdens concerns the precise definition of national output with which public expenditure and tax revenues are compared. There are at least three plausible ways of measuring money GDP, for example.[14] The chosen option can make a noticeable difference to the ratios concerned.

Arguably, the worst measure is GDP at market prices, which is reported gross of indirect taxes and subsidies, and overstates national output as a result. If a tax is added to a product, it increases the measured output of the economy at market prices totally artificially (and the opposite happens for a subsidy). Even so, it is the concept employed by the OECD and it is the officially preferred measure in Britain. This is partly for no better reason than that the figures are easier to compile, however. One drawback of market-price GDP is that the varying mixtures of direct and indirect taxes between countries mean that this measure distorts the relative rankings of the economies concerned.[15]

---

13 Readers who want more detail might like to know that there is a monthly-updated Excel spreadsheet published by the ONS on its website the working day following the release of the ONS *Public Sector Finances Statistical Bulletin*. This contains detailed quarterly data back to 1946 Q1, allowing both calendar and fiscal year data to be downloaded.

14 There is also a tradition of using net domestic product in some of the literature on 'tax-freedom' day, which subtracts capital depreciation from GDP. Conceptually, this is correct but is not widely employed because the capital depreciation figures are notoriously unreliable. However, the use of gross domestic product clearly biases downwards estimates of the tax and spending burdens, particularly now that short-lived software development is included as gross capital formation in the official figures.

15 For example, the VAT-heavy EU economies are probably being flattered by the market-price measure in comparison with, say, the US, where the overall tax burden is lower and possibly less reliant on indirect taxation.

Table 3   General government transactions by subsector and economic
category in fiscal 2015/16

	£bn	%	Ratio to GDP at market prices (%)	Ratio to GDP at factor cost (%)
Current expenditure				
Current consumption of goods and services	361.4	48.4	19.2	21.9
Subsidies	12.0	1.6	0.6	0.7
Net social benefits	230.8	30.9	12.3	14.0
Net current grants overseas	2.9	0.4	0.2	0.2
Other current grants	20.3	2.7	1.1	1.2
Debt interest	45.7	6.1	2.4	2.8
Payments to European Union	15.3	2.1	0.8	0.9
Capital expenditure				
Fixed investment	45.8	6.1	2.4	2.8
Stocks	−0.1	−0.0	−0.0	−0.0
Capital grants	13.2	1.8	0.7	0.8
Total expenditure	747.3	100.0	39.8	45.3
Receipts				
Taxes on income and wealth	220.9	32.8	11.8	13.4
Taxes on production	242.4	36.0	12.9	14.7
Compulsory social contributions	113.4	16.9	6.0	6.9
Other taxes	46.4	6.9	2.5	2.8
Non-oil taxes	623.1	92.6	33.2	37.8
Rent, interest and dividends	49.7	7.4	2.6	3.0
Total receipts	672.8	100.0	35.8	40.8
Net borrowing	74.5		4.0	4.5

Source: UK Office for National Statistics *Public Sector Finances* (Table PSA10) and *Quarterly National Accounts* 'Statistical Bulletins' released in June 2016. Calculations used data rounded to nearest £m, not £bn. North Sea tax revenues were effectively zero (minus £25m) in 2015/16.

Another is that market-price GDP increases – and the reported public spending ratio declines – when there is a revenue-neutral switch from direct to indirect taxation, even if underlying

Figure 4 Ratios of UK general government expenditure to GDP measured at both market prices and at factor cost 1870–2015

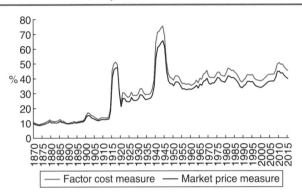

national output has not changed – and this has happened in the UK over time.[16]

The alternative measure of GDP 'at factor cost' excludes all indirect taxes and subsidies. As a result, it is arguably the most appropriate yardstick and it was widely accepted as being the best measure before the 1970s. The factor-cost measure has been adopted for the long-term historical comparisons that follow because it is not distorted by changes in the indirect tax burden over time. As can be seen from Figure 4, this distortion is particularly marked if comparisons are being made with the far lower tax and spending ratios that prevailed before World Wars I and II, for example. Figure 5 shows the percentage of national income by which the factor-cost measure of the government spending burden exceeds the one based on market price. It can be seen that this difference has increased over time and, as a result, the

---

16 Both the Thatcher government in 1979 and the Coalition in 2010 sharply increased VAT, with the result that any apparent cuts in the burdens of spending and taxation partly resulted from a change in the denominator not the numerator. Exaggerating the severity of fiscal retrenchment was politically convenient for both the Conservative and Labour parties, albeit for different reasons, on both occasions.

Figure 5   Differences between factor-cost and market-price measures of the UK spending burden 1870–2015

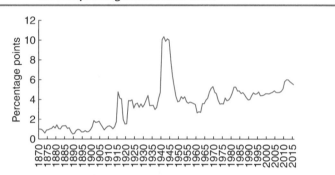

official understating of the government spending burden has increased.

As far as the UK specifically is concerned, factor-cost GDP has been given less prominence in recent years than the 'hybrid GDP' at basic prices, which is often referred to as gross value added (GVA). Basic-price GDP is used to measure regional GDP, for example, and excludes most, but not all, indirect taxes. Though this is not as satisfactory as GDP at factor cost, it is preferable to GDP at market prices. The trends in the government spending ratio using factor-cost and basic-price GDP are similar, because the two definitions are reasonably close. However, the government spending and tax burdens come out some 0.5–1.0 per cent lower using basic-price GDP as the denominator than when the better factor-cost GDP measure is used.

That the precise measure of national output used to quantify the burden of public spending is not just a trivial accounting point was revealed in the final two columns of Table 3 and is confirmed by Table 4, which shows that market-price GDP was nearly £229bn (13.9 per cent) higher than the factor-cost measure in 2015/16, and that the share of total general government expenditure (GGE) in money GDP was 39.8 per cent if the market-price

Table 4   Alternative measures of the shares of government spending and taxes in UK national output in fiscal year 2015/16

	Value (£bn)	Share of GGE in GDP (%)	Share of receipts in GDP (%)	Share of taxes and NICs in GDP (%)
General government expenditure (GGE)	747.3			
Total receipts	672.8			
Taxes and NICs	623.1			
GDP at current market prices	1,879.3	39.8	35.8	33.2
GDP at basic prices	1,673.6	44.7	40.2	37.2
GDP at factor cost	1,650.5	45.3	40.8	37.8
Non-oil GDP at current market prices	1,855.0	40.3	36.3	33.6
Non-oil GDP at basic prices	1,649.3	45.3	40.8	37.8
Non-oil GDP at factor cost	1,626.2	46.0	41.4	38.3

Source: UK Office for National Statistics *Public Sector Finances* and *Quarterly National Accounts* 'Statistical Bulletins' released in June 2016.

measure is employed and 45.3 per cent using factor-cost GDP, representing a substantial difference of 5.5 percentage points. Thus, when we hear the government or the media quote government spending ratios, they are dramatically understating the best estimates of the burden of government. Furthermore, the use of the market-price measure understates the increase in the ratio of government spending over time.

The national accounts revolution: ESA 2010

Something that has caused serious problems for all UK data users has been the scale of methodological changes to previous official statistics for the government sector and GDP in recent years, as the ONS has struggled to make Britain's national accounts consistent with the latest EU standards. This rewriting of history reached a crescendo when the ESA 2010 national accounts were introduced in the autumn of 2014 and were described as a 'once-in-a-generation' set of changes at the time. However, this statement did not prevent the ONS from implementing further major changes in September 2015 and again in June 2016. The extent of this rewriting of the past is illustrated by Table 5. This reveals the amendments to the official figures for the main expenditure components of money GDP in the year of 2013 following the switch to ESA 2010 in September 2014, the further methodological changes introduced in September 2015, and the most recent changes in June 2016.[17]

The original introduction of ESA 2010 in September 2014 was accompanied by large changes to the previous ONS data for the government finances. General government net borrowing (GGNB) in 2000/01 was revised up by £22.6bn, for example, and the figure for 2012/13 by £42bn. These dramatic changes resulted from a retrospective change in the treatment of the receipts from the 3G wireless spectrum auction and the transfer of the Post Office Pension Fund liabilities, respectively. In addition, there were revisions to a wide range of individual public spending and receipt items, sometimes going back over many decades.

These methodological innovations suggest that the Parliamentary debate on tax and spend issues has often been based on subsequently invalidated fiscal statistics. However, much of this political debate was concerned with the share of government expenditure and taxes in money GDP, which has itself been revised substantially. The cumulative increase of not far short of £127bn in money GDP between the ESA 1995 estimates published in June

---

17 There is a mystery concerning the June 2016 national accounts. While the start and end points of 1948 and 2015 are not too dissimilar to their forerunner, the ratio of the new series to the old seems to peak in the mid 1980s, with the new figures some 8 or 9 percentage points higher than in the previous official estimates. This has caused substantial downwards changes (of up to 2.7 percentage points) to the calculated spending and tax ratios during the years of peak revisions. The reason appears to have been a revised treatment of imputed rents from the ownership of property. Hughes (2016) provides more details.

2014 and the latest ESA 2010 figure[18] would have reduced the reported share of government spending in GDP in the historic year of 2013/14 by between 3.1 and 4 percentage points on its own, depending on the GDP definition employed. However, this was partly offset because ESA 2010 also introduced a new £16bn item into the government spending identity 'VAT and Gross National Income based EU contributions' (see Table 3), which picked up money paid directly to Brussels. Such payments were previously ignored in the UK government accounts.

The net effect of all the changes introduced since the last ESA 1995 figures were published has been to raise total general government expenditure in the fiscal year 2013/14, for example, from £707.7bn on the old measure to £733.9bn on the latest official figures (Table 6). However, the accompanying definitional increase in money GDP meant that the ratio of total spending to basic-price GDP, for example, dropped from 49.1 per cent to 46.9 per cent, representing a fall of 2.2 percentage points. The cash value of total receipts in 2013/14 was raised from £611.6bn to £629.9bn as a result of all the revisions introduced since June 2014. However, the ratio to basic-price GDP dropped from 42.5 per cent to 40.2 per cent because of the switch, representing a drop of 2.3 percentage points.

More generally, Table 6 indicates that the introduction of ESA 2010 and subsequent revisions reduced the reported government spending share by some 1.6–2.3 percentage points, depending on the precise GDP definition employed, with an even larger downgrading observable in the case of tax receipts of 2.2–2.9 percentage points. The spending proposals of the three major parties in the 2015 election debate differed by trivial amounts compared to the scale of these data amendments.

---

18 Just over £100bn came in with the implementation of ESA 2010 in September 2014 and the rest subsequently. It is possible to separate out the three stages of changes to the data using the figures given in Tables 5 and 6. However, it simplifies the text and tables if the three sets of changes are consolidated.

Table 5   Expenditure components of money GDP by value in 2013, as reported originally and as subsequently revised

	Old ESA 1995 figures released 30/6/14 (£bn)	ESA 2010 figures released 30/9/14 (£bn)	Subsequent ESA 2010 data released 30/9/15 (£bn)	Latest data released 30/6/2016 (£bn)	Difference between 30/6/16 and ESA 1995 figures (£bn)	Difference between 30/6/16 and ESA 1995 figures (%)
Household consumption	1,031.8	1,059.1	1,073.1	1,084.0	52.2	5.1
Non-profit institutions	39.1	51.7	55.0	54.5	15.4	39.4
Government consumption	343.2	346.8	348.2	349.6	6.4	1.9
Gross fixed capital formation	225.8	281.5	280.5	280.2	54.4	24.1
Change in inventories	7.9	8.8	7.2	5.1	−2.8	−35.4
Valuation changes	1.8	1.4	5.4	5.3	3.5	194.4
Exports	505.6	511.3	521.0	517.6	12.0	2.4
Gross final expenditure	2,155.2	2,260.6	2,290.2	2,296.4	141.2	6.6
Imports	534.1	543.4	555.3	556.8	22.7	4.3
Statistical discrepancy	−8.4	−3.9	0.0	0.0	8.4	n/a
GDP at market prices	1,612.8	1,713.3	1734.9	1,739.6	126.8	7.9
Basic price adjustment	188.1	188.0	188.0	188.0	−0.1	−0.1
GDP at basic prices	1,424.7	1,525.3	1,546.9	1,551.6	126.9	8.9

Source: UK Office for National Statistics *Quarterly National Accounts,* June 2014, September 2014, September 2015 and June 2016. Gross final expenditure equals the sum of the rows above. Imports and the basic price adjustment are then subtracted to define GDP at market prices and at basic prices, respectively.

These statistical changes also render it almost impossible to evaluate how far the former Chancellor, Mr Osborne, achieved the goals he set out in 2010 without a major exercise in forensic accounting.

Table 6   Comparison of UK government spending and tax ratios in fiscal
           2013/14 using four different generations of official data

	Original June 2014 ESA 1995 measure	Revised September 2014 ESA 2010 measure	Further revised December 2015 ESA 2010 measure	Latest (June 2016) estimate	Cumulated difference June 2016 less ESA 1995 measure
£ billion					
GDP at market prices	1,631.4	1,732.4	1,755.9	1,757.2	125.8
GDP at factor cost	1,417.8	1,518.4	1,539.8	1,542.1	124.3
GDP at basic prices	1,440.1	1,541.1	1,564.5	1,565.8	125.7
Government spending	707.7	726.9	733.6	733.9	26.2
Non-oil taxes	568.9	571.0	574.1	574.3	5.4
Ratios to GDP at market prices (%)					
Government spending	43.4	42.0	41.8	41.8	−1.6
Non-oil taxes	34.9	33.0	32.7	32.7	−2.2
Ratios to GDP at factor cost (%)					
Government spending	49.9	47.9	47.6	47.6	−2.3
Non-oil taxes	40.1	37.6	37.3	37.2	−2.9
Ratios to GDP at basic prices (%)					
Government spending	49.1	47.2	46.9	46.9	−2.2
Non-oil taxes	39.5	37.1	36.7	36.7	−2.8

Source: UK Office for National Statistics *Quarterly National Accounts*, June 2014, September 2014,
September 2015 and June 2016 and *Public Sector Finances* 'Statistical Bulletins', for corresponding
dates.

Is there a best buy?

These statistical issues are important. They lead to material
changes in our estimates of national income, government spending and taxation and in the ratios of any one of the variables

to the others. Making comparisons over time without properly understanding the data leads to widely misleading statements being made, such as that by the BBC journalist who described the 2014 budget as taking us back to the land of *The Road to Wigan Pier* (in terms of the level of government spending in relation to GDP). However unreasonable that statement was, it should be noted that it was based on an equally misleading statement that came from a government body.

Crudely, we can say that there are two types of problem when examining national income and government spending statistics. Firstly, there are technical differences of the type discussed immediately above – for example, how we calculate imputed rent on property within GDP figures or whether the movement of pension liabilities onto the state balance sheet should constitute government spending. These will always be difficult to resolve and new information, improved measurement techniques or a better understanding of the underlying theory may well lead to revisions. Secondly, there are conceptual issues such as whether national income should be measured at factor cost or market prices – these questions have more objective answers. As has been noted above, the most appropriate ratios to use to measure the underlying tax burden are those that relate government spending (whether financed by current taxation or borrowing) to GDP at factor cost. GDP at basic prices, where factor-cost measures are not available, is a reasonable alternative.

When looking at how to determine the burden of taxation and government spending, there is a further question. Should we be concerned about the government/private spending ratio rather than just the share of government spending in GDP (irrespective of how GDP is defined)?

It was argued in Smith (2006) that, because it was conceptually impossible for the state to fund itself, more relevant measures of the tax and spending burdens were their ratios to the non-socialised element of national output. Essentially, the argument was that, if a taxpayer carries one bureaucrat (or welfare recipient) on his or her back, the ratio is 'one to one',[19] not 'one to one plus one', and that, if the taxpayer carries two bureaucrats, the ratio is 'two to one', not 'two over three', and so on.

Likewise, expressing fiscal deficits as a share of total GDP can give a misleading indication of fiscal irresponsibility. Because government cannot absorb its own debt – only the domestic private sector and overseas residents can do that – funding a budget deficit becomes increasingly difficult as the share of the private sector in GDP declines. The same applies to the stock of government debt, where it is the ratio to non-socialised GDP that is the crucial indicator of fiscal sustainability. Public choice theory suggests that official data are produced by bureaucrats and politicians to put the best possible spin on their own activities, rather than to enlighten the citizenry.[20] This is probably why politicians and officials seem to plump for definitions that reduce the reported tax and spending burdens, irrespective of the economic merits of the measures concerned.

---

19 This situation corresponds to the 100 per cent line in Figure 3.

20 The January–March 2012 issue of *World Economics*, Volume 13, Number 1, is largely devoted to *The Dire State of Government Accounting Practices*. The title of the contribution by Ball and Pflugraph (2012), '*Making Enron Look Good*', conveys the flavour of the analysis.

3 HISTORICAL TRENDS IN THE GOVERNMENT SPENDING AND TAX RATIOS

David B. Smith

The international experience

It was suggested earlier that the 'least-bad' estimates for international comparisons were those provided by the OECD, despite the fact that these used market-price GDP as the scaling factor. Nevertheless, the OECD figures have the advantages that they are reworked onto a consistent basis and the results are conveniently obtainable in the Annex tables to the OECD's twice-yearly *Economic Outlook* from 1997 onwards, with longer back-runs available in the OECD's data bank.

The author has published long-run figures for the share of general government spending in market-price GDP in the industrialised economies on several previous occasions (e.g. Smith 2006, 2014). In the past, the method employed was to update the historical figures that commenced in the late nineteenth century given in Table 1.1 of Tanzi and Schuknecht (2000) using the latest available OECD figures.[1] The most recent such update, which employs the June 2016 OECD *Economic Outlook,* appears in Table 7. Unfortunately, national accounting conventions have changed noticeably since Tanzi and Schuknecht performed their ground-breaking research sixteen years ago. As a consequence, there are serious discrepancies between the spending ratios that

---

1 Tanzi did the same in Tanzi (2011).

they provide for 1996 – the final year covered in their book – and the latest OECD figures. At the extremes, the government spending ratio for New Zealand in 1996 has been revised up by 5.5 percentage points in the June 2016 OECD report and that for Austria by 4.4 percentage points, while the ratio for Switzerland has been cut by 5 percentage points. The latest US figure for the 1996 overlap year is 4.1 percentage points higher in the current OECD report than in Tanzi and Schuknecht, while the equivalent British figure has been revised down by 3.1 percentage points.

These discontinuities mean that the figures in Table 7 should be regarded as no better than rough-and-ready approximations as the figures up to and including 1960 are not consistent with those from 1980 onwards. Nevertheless, the broad picture is clear – there have been huge upwards shifts in the spending ratios since the late nineteenth century. Furthermore, and fortuitously, the changes to the figures after 1996 for the twelve countries for which continuous data exist average out at reasonably close to zero (specifically, there is a relatively modest *minus* 0.8 percentage points adjustment arising from the revisions because of offsetting breaks). This average suggests that the 'typical' industrialised state was spending slightly more than one tenth of national output before the 1914–18 war – a period that can be regarded as the heyday of genuine free-market capitalist economies – between a fifth and a third or so in the late 1930s, when Keynes published his *General Theory,* between one quarter and one third in 1960, and some 45 per cent in 2015 on a break-corrected basis.

The available figures for the aggregate OECD spending ratio started in 1960 and measured 30.3 per cent, although it then rose noticeably between the mid 1960s and mid 1970s – partly as a result of the Vietnam War and President Johnson's Great Society welfare programmes in the US and the emergence of a new generation of big-spending politicians elsewhere in the West. However, the spending ratio subsequently increased more slowly to reach

Table 7   Ratios of general government expenditure, including transfers, to money GDP at market prices (%)

	1870	1913	1920	1937	1960	1980	2000	2010	2015
Australia	18.3	16.5	19.3	14.8	21.2	34.1	34.6	36.6	35.6
Austria	10.5	17.0	14.7	20.6	36.3	49.2	50.2	52.8	51.7
Belgium	—	13.8	—	21.8	30.3	57.3	49.0	53.3	54.0
Canada	—	—	16.7	25.0	28.6	41.1	40.7	43.2	40.3
France	12.6	17.0	27.6	29.0	34.6	46.1	51.1	56.4	57.0
Germany	10.0	14.8	25.0	34.1	32.4	47.9	44.7	47.4	44.0
Italy	13.7	17.1	30.1	31.1	30.1	40.1	45.4	49.9	50.5
Ireland	—	—	—	-	28.0	48.9	30.9	65.7	35.2
Japan	8.8	8.3	14.8	25.4	17.5	33.1	38.8	40.7	41.3
Netherlands	9.1	9.0	13.5	19.0	33.7	53.4	41.8	48.2	44.9
New Zealand	—	—	24.6	25.3	26.9	38.1	37.5	47.8	41.9
Norway	5.9	9.3	16.0	11.8	29.9	45.6	42.0	45.0	48.6
Spain	—	8.3	9.3	18.4	18.8	34.2	39.1	45.6	43.3
Sweden	5.7	10.4	10.9	16.5	31.0	57.7	53.6	51.3	50.4
Switzerland	16.5	14.0	17.0	24.1	17.2	32.8	34.2	32.9	34.0
UK	9.4	12.7	26.2	30.0	32.2	44.7	37.8	48.8	43.2
USA	7.3	7.5	12.1	19.4	30.0	35.3	33.9	43.2	37.8
OECD	n/a	n/a	n/a	n/a	30.3	39.4	38.7	44.0	41.2
Average for 12 countries with no missing figures:									
	10.7	12.8	19.9	23.0	28.8	43.3	42.3	46.1	44.9

Sources: Tanzi and Schuknecht (2000), OECD Economic Outlook (June 2016, Annex Table 29), and OECD data bank.

39.4 per cent by 1980 (Figure 6). Following two decades of little net change, the OECD spending ratio increased from 38.7 per cent in 2000 to a peak of 44.5 per cent in 2009 before easing to 41.2 per cent in 2015. This average conceals a huge divergence within the total, however, with Korea having a spending ratio of 32.9 per cent in 2015 at the bottom end (with Switzerland and Australia at 34 per cent and 35.6 per cent, respectively) and Denmark and Finland having ratios of 55.7 per cent and 58.3 per cent at the top.

Figure 6   Aggregate OECD government spending and revenues expressed as a share of GDP at market prices 1960–2015

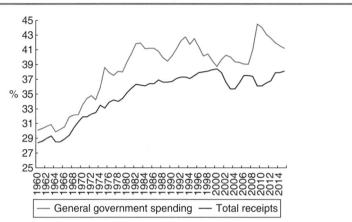

— General government spending   — Total receipts

Despite the furore over the alleged spending cuts implemented in Britain since 2010, the UK has been a consistently bigger spender than the OECD norm over much of the past five-and-a-half decades, apart from between 1988 and 2001 (see Figure 7). This exceptional period possibly reflected Lady Thatcher's reforms in the 1980s and the relatively cautious fiscal policies adopted in the first three years of the Blair Labour government.

Unfortunately, it is not possible to obtain estimates of the tax burden as far back as the spending figures used in Table 7. Nevertheless, the conventional wisdom in favour of balanced budgets before the late 1950s suggests that the spending and tax burdens developed in parallel for much of that period, apart from during the two world wars and the Great Depression of the 1930s. Tanzi (2011: 92) has summarised the situation:

> There had been significant increases in the levels of taxation during World War I (to finance part of the huge spending for the war), followed by slow growth until World War II when, as happened in the First World War, but in larger amounts, taxes

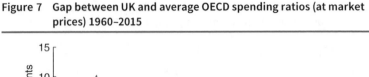

Figure 7 Gap between UK and average OECD spending ratios (at market prices) 1960–2015

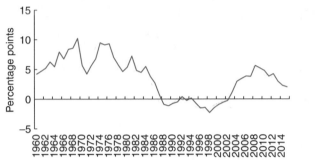

were increased to finance the new war. Tax levels for general government were only 11% of Gross National Product (GNP) in 1925–29 in the United States; 20% in France in 1924–25; and less than 10% until 1930 and still below 20% up to 1950 in Sweden. They were about 25% of GNP in 1924–25 and around 30% of GNP in the 1960s in the United Kingdom. In the United States, they were around 28% of GNP in the 1960s, a large increase from the 1920s. From the end of World War II until about 1960, there were relatively modest changes; tax levels remained low compared with the shares of GDP that they would reach in many other countries in later years. The fall of military spending after World War II accommodated some of the increase in civilian spending in some countries, including the United States.

The more recent period of rising tax burdens from 1965 onwards is well documented in the OECD's annual Revenue Statistics, which publishes figures for the ratio of general government tax receipts to market-price GDP for thirty-four OECD member countries. These figures appear in Table 8, which shows the same countries as Table 7. This reveals that the ratio of tax receipts to money GDP in the OECD area had increased from 24.8 per

Table 8   Ratios of total tax revenues to money GDP at market prices (%)

	1965	1970	1980	1990	2000	2010	2014
Australia	20.6	21.1	26.2	28.1	30.4	25.6	27.5*
Austria	33.6	33.7	38.7	39.4	42.1	40.8	43.0
Belgium	30.6	33.3	40.6	41.2	43.6	42.4	44.7
Canada	25.3	30.3	30.5	35.3	34.9	30.4	30.8
France	33.6	33.6	39.4	41.0	43.1	41.6	45.2
Germany	31.6	31.5	36.4	34.8	36.2	35.0	36.1
Italy	24.7	24.8	28.7	36.4	40.6	41.5	43.6
Ireland	24.5	27.6	30.1	32.4	30.9	27.5	29.9
Japan	17.8	19.2	24.8	28.5	26.6	27.6	30.3*
Netherlands	30.9	33.4	40.3	40.2	36.8	36.2	36.7*
New Zealand	23.2	25.1	29.6	36.2	32.5	30.6	32.4
Norway	29.4	34.3	41.9	40.2	41.9	41.9	39.1
Spain	14.3	15.5	22.0	31.6	33.4	29.9	33.2
Sweden	31.4	35.7	43.7	49.5	49.0	43.2	42.7
Switzerland	16.6	18.2	23.3	23.6	27.6	26.5	26.6
UK	29.3	35.0	33.4	32.9	34.7	32.8	32.6
USA	23.5	25.7	25.5	25.9	28.2	23.2	26.0
OECD	24.8	26.7	30.1	32.1	34.3	32.8	34.4

Source: OECD Revenue Statistics, December 2015, and databank.
*2013 not 2014.

cent in 1965 to 34.4 per cent in 2014, which is the latest published figure. The more timely figures for total receipts, which include the state's income from rent, interest and dividends were 28.5 per cent in 1965, 37.9 per cent in 2014 and 38.1 per cent in 2015 (Figure 6). However, there are once again substantial variations between countries. In 2015, general government receipts ranged from around one third of market-price GDP in Korea, the US, Switzerland and Australia to 38.8 per cent in the UK and an eye-watering 53.5 per cent in France, 53.6 per cent in Denmark, 54.4 per cent in Norway and 55.5 per cent in Finland.

However, the published tax ratios need to be treated with some caution because they do not necessarily provide a reliable indicator of the absolute or relative tax burdens being placed on an economy. One reason is that tax receipts tend to be more cyclical than economic activity, reflecting the fact that the private-sector tax base is more cyclically volatile than total GDP and also the progressive nature of the tax system. This means that an apparent fall in the tax-to-GDP ratio may not reflect a reduction in the various rates of tax but, instead, either that the country is in recession or that an increased socialised sector has crowded out the private-sector tax base.

It has also been accepted in the public finance literature for well over a century that excessive marginal rates of particular taxes reduce receipts, even if there is slightly more debate as to whether this applies at an aggregated level to produce an adverse Laffer curve effect.[2] In this situation, a decline in the tax ratio can reflect an excessive tax burden, not its easing. This also applies in reverse. The fiscal stabilisation literature (Smith 2006: 106–9) suggests that bold policies of tax cutting and supply side reform are frequently followed by an unexpected surge in receipts, which is more marked than the accompanying rise in activity.

A final health warning is that the aggregate OECD receipts ratios appear to have been revised downwards in recent years, presumably because of the new national accounting conventions described above and perhaps also because of the admission of new members to the organisation. This means that published

---

2   By chance, the author has in his possession the 1917 edition of C. F. Bastable's *Public Finance*, the first edition of which appeared in 1892. This not only explains why higher rates of tax will reduce receipts beyond a certain point but also discusses whether this property applies in aggregate, i.e. whether there is a macro as well as a micro Laffer curve. Unfortunately, the forecasting methodology formerly employed by HM Treasury and currently by the Office for Budget Responsibility seems to implicitly make the assumption that there is no impact of a change in tax rates on the private-sector tax base as, arguably, does some of the macroeconomic analysis carried out by the Institute for Fiscal Studies.

empirical studies may not be a reliable guide to the sustainable share of taxes in GDP, for example. In particular, the latest figures for the OECD as a whole in 1970 and 1980 appear to be some 2.5 percentage points lower than those published a few years ago.

The British experience 1870–2015

The UK is fortunate in that its national accounts have been well documented on a calendar year basis well before 1948, when the official ONS figures commence. These data exist because of the pioneering work of economic historians such as the late Charles Feinstein (1972). The Bank of England has mounted many of these data series on its website, in some cases back to the seventeenth century, making the data readily available.[3] A major difficulty in compiling consistently defined back runs for the UK tax and spending ratios, therefore, is not a paucity of historic data but the instability of the recent ONS figures. The least bad solution, if consistently defined data series are required, is to link the historic pre-ONS data onto the current official definitions using chain-linking.[4] However, this has the nonsensical consequence that the calculated public spending ratio in, say, 1913 or 1938 can change every year because the ONS has altered the way it assembles the national accounts from 1948 onwards.[5]

---

3 See www.bankofengland.co.uk/research/Pages/onebank/threecenturies.aspx. For more information, see Hills et al. (2010).

4 To be precise, the author has used the Bank's figures for all three measures of money GDP from 1870 to 1947 but scaled them where appropriate to be consistent with the ONS data from 1948 onwards. On previous occasions, the author has largely worked with Feinstein's historic data, which were also employed by the Bank. 'Chain linking' means multiplying the earlier data by the ratio of the revised data to the old series in the earliest common year; in this case, that was 1948.

5 The cumulated shifts over several years of redefinitions are noticeable and can amount to several percentage points. As noted above, the reworked national accounts released on 30 June 2016 have led to substantial revisions to the spending and tax ratios in parts of the post-1948 period.

Fortunately, the government accounts appear to be rather more robust than the GDP figures and government subsidies, national insurance contributions and direct tax receipts are all examples of where zero or only trivial scaling adjustments have been required. The most drastic data surgery that has been undertaken for Table 9 has been to aggregate general government current consumption of goods and services with 'other current grants', which appear to be predominantly payments to non-profit institutions acting as agents for the government. This distinction was not present in the historical data.

Table 9 shows the ratios of the main categories of UK general government expenditure and non-oil taxes to factor-cost GDP back to 1900 for taxes and back to 1870 for spending at a series of selected benchmark dates. The underlying annual data were also used to plot Figures 1–3 and Figures 8 and 9.

Table 9 reveals that the ratio of UK general government spending to factor-cost GDP had fluctuated between 10 and 15 per cent between 1870 and World War I, apart from a brief spike that reached 17.2 per cent in 1901 caused by the Boer War. The spending ratio then peaked at 51.1 per cent in 1917, during World War I, before dropping to 22.9 per cent in 1920 as wartime expenditures were cut back. The UK spending burden then spent much of the interwar period fluctuating between 27.5 and 33.7 per cent, before hitting a record 75.6 per cent in 1944, when World War II was at its high point.

Government spending from Churchill to Thatcher

Spending then reached a post-war low point of 36.5 per cent of GDP in 1955, following the well-considered, and often overlooked, supply-side reforms implemented by the post-war Churchill administration's Chancellor of the Exchequer, R. A. Butler (Smith

2012), which ushered in the post-war 'Golden Age'.[6] After that, the spending ratio started a steady upwards climb, firstly, under the paternalist Conservative administration of Harold Macmillan and subsequently during the 1964–70 Labour administration. The latter saw the spending ratio peak at 45.5 per cent in 1969 when the UK had to be bailed out by the International Monetary Fund (IMF). The government spending ratio fell to 40.5 per cent in 1973 during the Heath–Barber credit boom of the early 1970s, but then rose rapidly as a result of the big spending policies of the Labour government that took office in 1974. The spending ratio peaked at 44.4 per cent in 1976, at the end of which the UK again had to borrow from the IMF.

The Thatcher period and beyond

In 1979, Lady Thatcher inherited a spending ratio of 41.6 per cent. However, this rose to 47 per cent during the recession of 1981 before falling to 39 per cent by 1990, when she left office. Britain's membership of the Exchange Rate Mechanism (ERM), and the accompanying recession, saw the government spending ratio peak at 42.6 per cent in 1992, when sterling was ejected from the ERM, but the ratio was down to 39.2 per cent when New Labour took office in 1997. This figure declined to 38.5 per cent in 2000, during Gordon Brown's flirtation with 'prudence', but had already risen to 42.9 per cent in 2007, before the global financial crash. The subsequent recession, together with the costs of the bank bailouts, meant that the spending ratio had climbed to

---

6 During the twelve years 1953–1964, UK economic growth averaged 3.6 per cent; real household consumption increased at an annual average of 3.7 per cent; retail price inflation averaged 3 per cent (the equivalent of just over 2 per cent on the modern CPI); claimant unemployment averaged 408,000 or 1.4 per cent; general government net borrowing averaged a modest 0.5 per cent of GDP; and the balance of payments current account was in surplus for all but three years.

Table 9 Ratios of main categories of UK general government expenditure plus taxes to money GDP at factor cost (%)

	Government final current expenditure	Net social benefits	Subsidies	Debt interest	Government investment, capital grants and funds paid to European Union	Total general government expenditure	All tax receipts
1870	5.8	0.0	0.0	3.9	1.0	10.7	n/a
1900	10.9	0.3	0.0	1.9	2.5	15.6	8.8
1910	9.7	0.5	0.0	2.1	1.6	13.9	10.7
1920	9.6	2.6	2.3	6.4	2.0	22.9	21.4
1930	11.7	5.3	0.6	8.8	3.6	30.0	22.1
1938	16.8	5.3	0.8	6.0	4.2	33.1	24.2
1950	20.2	5.8	4.1	4.8	4.0	38.9	38.8
1960	18.5	6.1	2.0	4.3	4.5	35.4	29.8
1970	19.1	8.0	1.8	4.2	8.6	41.7	38.9
1980	21.9	10.4	2.2	4.9	4.6	44.0	35.7
1990	19.3	10.0	0.8	3.4	5.5	39.0	34.1
2000	20.4	11.5	0.4	2.7	3.5	38.5	37.4
2010	26.4	14.4	0.7	3.3	5.8	50.6	37.5
Wartime peaks							
1917	43.2	1.0	0.6	4.8	1.5	51.1	17.3
1944	62.1	5.3	2.9	5.3	0.0	75.6	41.8

Continued

	Government final current expenditure	Net social benefits	Subsidies	Debt interest	Government investment, capital grants and funds paid to European Union	Total general government expenditure	All tax receipts
Recent years							
2011	25.5	14.5	0.6	3.6	5.4	49.6	38.5
2012	25.3	14.8	0.6	3.3	5.7	49.7	37.6
2013	24.3	14.5	0.6	3.2	5.1	47.7	37.5
2014	23.7	14.2	0.6	3.1	4.8	46.4	37.0
2015	23.2	14.0	0.7	2.7	4.8	45.4	37.5
Scaled OBR budget forecasts							
2015/16	23.0	14.0	0.8	2.8	4.7	45.3	37.9
2016/17	22.6	13.5	0.9	2.8	5.0	44.8	38.5
2017/18	22.2	13.1	0.9	2.9	4.7	43.8	38.6
2018/19	21.5	12.7	1.0	3.0	4.7	42.9	38.6
2019/20	20.9	12.4	1.1	2.9	4.4	41.7	39.1
2020/21	20.4	12.2	1.1	2.7	5.0	41.4	38.8

Sources: Feinstein (1972), Bank of England and ONS databanks and Office for Budget Responsibility *Economic and Fiscal Outlook*, March 2016, Supplementary Fiscal Table 2.38. Note: 'other current grants' have been consolidated with 'government final expenditure' to maintain consistency with historic figures. The figures for 1900 and 1950 are distorted by the Boer War and the Korean War, respectively. Note: in order to maintain consistency with the historic figures, the OBR Budget Forecasts have been scaled down by the ratio of the OBR's figure for GDP at factor cost in 2015/16 (£1,643.3bn) to the revised post-June 2016 measure (£1,650.5bn) to give a scaling factor of 0.9956. This typically reduces the OBR's figures for total spending and taxes by 0.2 percentage points and the figures for current expenditure and social benefits by 0.1 percentage points.

Figure 8 Ratio of UK general government current expenditure to GDP at factor cost 1870–2015

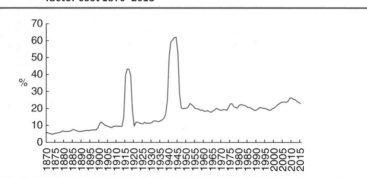

50.6 per cent at its peak in 2010, before falling to 45.4 per cent in 2015 and 45 per cent in the four quarters ending in 2016 Q2.

The components of government spending

Looking more closely at the components of government spending, Figure 8 shows the share of national output absorbed by general government current expenditure from 1870 onwards. Current expenditure represents not quite one half of total general government expenditure, and contains two essential elements: the public sector salary bill and procurement of goods and services. It is expenditure on the latter that might be expected to have the strongest Keynesian multiplier effects. This is because it injects demand directly into the private economy, if it is not offset by higher taxes.

Figure 9 illustrates the long-term decline in debt interest payments from the peak observed after World War I together with the seemingly inexorable rise of welfare payments after 1960, from negligible before 1914 to 14 per cent of factor-cost GDP currently.

Figure 9 Ratio of UK general government debt interest and welfare payments to UK GDP at factor cost 1870–2015

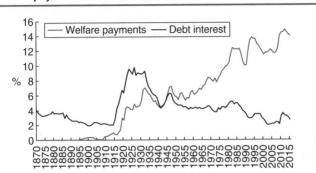

Regional breakdown of UK government spending

Modern Britain possesses an economy in which there are marked differences between the regions. How to compile regional government spending ratios was discussed in Chapter 5 of Smith (2006)[7] and that material will not be repeated here. However, Table 10 shows the estimated ratios of government spending to all three measures of regional GDP in 2012/13. This is the latest year for which a regional spending breakdown is presently available.

Apart from being out of date, there are other caveats about the figures. One is that the regional GDP data now only seem to be available on a workforce basis, whereas formerly residence-based figures were also available.

An additional measurement complication is that the published regional figures for GDP contain an 'ex regio' component – which is regionally unallocated employment and capital

---

7   More up-to-date figures for regional government spending ratios for 2009/10 were presented in Table 8 of Smith (2011: 57). However, these were based on the previous ESA 1995 national accounts conventions and cannot be compared with the current (June 2016) ESA 2010 figures.

Table 10 UK general government expenditure in 2012/13 by country and region on a residence basis

	Scaled public spending 2012/13 (£m)	Estimated GDP at basic prices 2012/13 (£m)	Ratio to GDP at basic prices (%)	Ratio to GDP at factor cost (%)	Ratio to GDP at market prices (%)	Public sector employment in 2016 Q1 (%)	Workless households in 2014 (%)	GVA per head in 2014 (£)
North East	31,894	45,380	69.7	70.8	62.3	20.3	21.7	18,216
North West	85,280	140,925	60.0	60.9	53.6	18.0	20.0	21,011
Yorkshire and Humber	59,564	102,030	57.9	58.8	51.7	18.6	17.7	19,863
East Midlands	48,248	89,179	53.6	54.4	47.9	15.4	15.5	20,524
West Midlands	62,395	109,951	56.2	57.1	50.2	17.2	18.2	20,086
Eastern England	60,450	130,256	46.0	46.7	41.1	15.3	12.7	23,063
London	102,001	335,823	30.1	30.6	26.9	14.3	14.6	42,666
South East	86,709	227,875	37.7	38.3	33.7	15.0	12.6	27,012
South West	57,101	113,724	49.8	50.6	44.5	16.5	13.8	22,324
England	593,642	1,295,144	45.4	46.1	40.6	16.2	15.8	25,367
Scotland	70,191	117,388	59.3	60.2	53.0	20.8	18.3	23,102
Wales	38,838	51,809	74.3	75.4	66.4	21.3	19.4	17,573
Northern Ireland	25,808	33,461	76.5	77.7	68.3	25.3	21.4	18,682
UK	728,478	1,497,801	48.2	48.9	43.1	17.0	16.4	24,616

Source: HM Treasury Public Expenditure Statistical Analysis 2014, 1 August 2015, Office for National Statistics Regional Gross Value Added (Income Approach), 1997 to 2014, 9 December 2015, Public Employment Statistical Bulletin, 15th June 2016 and Workless Households for Regions across the UK, 6 October 2015. A workless household contains at least one person aged 16–64 where no one aged 16 or over is in employment.

incomes and amounted to £23.7bn in 2012 – while there is almost £169bn (i.e. 23.2 per cent) of government spending that cannot be allocated on a regional UK basis. In both cases, the individual regional figures have been scaled proportionately so that they sum to equal the corresponding national totals. Another caveat is that the regional GDP figures are measured at basic prices and on a calendar-year basis but the expenditure data are on a financial year basis. To get round this problem, the 2012 calendar year regional GDP data have been rescaled to total the UK figure for 2012/13.

As discussed earlier, the basic-price and factor-cost ratios shown in Table 10 arguably provide the best measure of the socialisation of the various regions. However, the market-price measures in the fifth column can be compared with the international figures given in Table 7. This comparison needs to be treated with caution, however, because (1) the two sets of figures are not totally consistent, while (2) the UK-wide ratio fell by more than 3 percentage points between 2012/13 and 2015/16.

As it is, a comparison of the UK market-price figures for 2012/13 with the OECD statistics for 2015 shows that the 41.4 percentage point gap between the spending ratio in London (26.9 per cent) and Northern Ireland (68.3 per cent) exceeds the 25.4 percentage point range observed within the OECD (that is, it is bigger than the gap between Korea at 32.9 per cent and Finland at 58.3 per cent). If London were a country, it would have the lowest spending ratio in the OECD. The South East would then come in at number 3, after Korea, while the Greater South East[8] at 31.8 per cent would still be 1.1 percentage points below Korea. At the other extreme, the North East (62.3 per cent) and Wales (66.4 per cent), as well as Northern Ireland, are all more socialised than any member country of the OECD. Scotland's 53 per cent spending ratio would make it the sixth most socialised OECD member but

---

8   London plus South Eastern and Eastern England.

still below Belgium (54 per cent), Greece (55.5 per cent), Denmark (55.7 per cent), France (57 per cent) and Finland.

Given the near 'iron-curtain' spending ratios in some of the UK's peripheral regions, it is ironical that their problems are still widely seen as a 'failure of capitalism' rather than as a 'failure of socialism' and that nobody challenges this myth. The underground – or free market – sector apparently accounted for around one quarter of Soviet GDP in the 1970s and rather more in some of its Eastern European satellites, such as Hungry. Above-quota agricultural production, private housebuilding, small mom-and-pop businesses and black-market activities existed to varying degrees in all the former Communist nations. If one assumes that the lower limit on the government spending ratio is 10 per cent, and the effective upper limit is 75 per cent, then it is possible to calculate how far along the spectrum from capitalism to socialism the various UK regions are using the market-price GDP measure. This calculation would put the Greater South East at 33.5 per cent and Northern Ireland at 89.7 per cent, with England overall at 47 per cent, Scotland at 66.2 per cent and Wales at 86.8 per cent.[9]

Deindustrialisation in a number of regions has been a major issue because it has led to a collapse in the demand for unskilled labour.[10] These problems are likely to be exacerbated by the introduction of Mr Osborne's living wage policy, which will have little bite in the Greater South East but could be devastatingly harmful in Wales or the North East, for example. Given their high spending ratios, a necessary condition for the regeneration of the

9   The formula employed was: (Regional spending ratio (%) – 10%)/65%.

10 Deindustrialisation has not just been an 'act of God'. Supply side theory suggests that the supply of goods and services that can be traded internationally – including manufactured products – will move from high tax to low tax economies over time. So, deindustrialisation is itself a symptom of an excessively large state, at least in relative terms. The coming on stream of South East Asian economies with spending ratios typically one half of those prevailing in the OECD has greatly exacerbated these effects.

UK's old industrial heartlands is almost certainly the sort of big-bang market-liberalisation reforms implemented by the more successful former Communist countries (see Havrylyshyn et al. 2016). Such reforms require more political courage than shunting large sums of taxpayers' money from the Greater South East to the heavily subsidised areas and then regulating wages. The public choice pressures probably mean that the subsidies will continue and the necessary reforms will not take place.

4 AND THEY CALL IT AUSTERITY[1]

Ryan Bourne

Introduction

Much political and economic discussion over the past five years has been focused on 'cuts' to government expenditure made by the coalition and Conservative governments. Since, in the long run, the government faces a hard budget constraint, government expenditure amounts to the true tax burden imposed on citizens of a country, since expenditure can only be financed by taxation directly, borrowing (deferred taxation) or through inflation (in effect, a tax on money holdings). For this reason, while there have been significant tax increases since 2010, the focus of this chapter will be on government spending.

In an attempt to first eliminate the structural current budget deficit, then to get the debt-to-GDP ratio under control and then, more recently, to achieve a surplus by 2020, both the coalition and Conservative governments have sought to stem the growth

---

1 For reasons outlined in previous chapters, as well as revisions to spending and tax totals arising from changing economic circumstances, the true recorded state of the public finances is ever-changing. Indeed, by the time this is published, the figures presented here are likely to be out of date, particularly if post-Brexit uncertainty leads to a slowing of economic growth. Unless otherwise stated, this chapter uses three sources to assess trends in public spending based around the most recent public figures as of July 2016. Those sources are the most recent spending totals published at a major fiscal event (Budget 2016), the most up-to-date GDP deflator (from the ONS in July 2016) and the most recent Public Expenditure Statistical Analyses (again, July 2016).

of government spending. This, in common parlance, has been referred to as 'austerity'.

As previous chapters of this book have shown, in historical terms overall government spending is still extraordinarily high, but it is certainly true that the coalition and Conservative governments have slightly reduced government spending in real terms since 2010/11 – a largely unprecedented achievement since the mid 1970s.

Yet there are many misconceptions about what has happened to government spending since the start of the last parliament. Public debate often exaggerates the scale of the overall cuts and a myth about the path of government spending over the past five years has taken hold.

The exaggeration of the scale of spending reductions arises largely as a result of people using what has happened to some *components* of public expenditure as a proxy for discussing what has happened to overall spending. Overall real spending only fell slightly in the last parliament between 2010/11 and 2014/15 (by 2.1 per cent), but this masks significant changes in the composition of spending which have seen some areas cut significantly, while other areas saw spending increases. This is due both to the government's decisions to ring-fence significant areas of spending and unforeseen changes to 'demand driven' areas of spending. Still, what has happened overall to government spending hardly warrants the term 'savage', which is often the word used to describe the small cuts that have occurred.

There is also a myth that the previous coalition government loosened public expenditure in the midst of weaker than expected economic growth in the last parliament, thus resorting to what became known as 'plan B' – that is, a Keynesian fiscal stimulus as demanded by their opponents. In fact, though the coalition government borrowed more than expected and the composition of spending was different due to weak productivity growth, the extra borrowing primarily arose due to tax revenues being much lower than expected. The government's spending ambitions in terms of the aggregate totals were largely achieved, though perhaps not in the way they were expecting.

This chapter aims to provide a simple overview of, first, what happened to government spending under the coalition government and, second, what is projected to happen to government spending under the current Conservative administration. The approach taken is to provide a number of simple metrics for a range of measures of expenditure: nominal terms; real terms; spending as a proportion of GDP; and real terms per capita spending. It will then analyse some of the compositional changes in expenditure that have been seen and that we expect in the future. Where possible, it will focus on changes in resources allocated to broad *functions* of governments, rather than to departments. This is a more meaningful economic approach given that many functions of government, such as education, are spread across a range of departments in Whitehall.

Government spending under the coalition

Overall spending versus plans

In its emergency 2010 budget, the incoming coalition government set out plans to increase public expenditure in cash terms between 2010/11 and 2014/15 from £696.8 billion to £737.5 billion (a nominal increase of 5.8 per cent).[2] Given expected inflation at the time, this plan projected a real-terms cut in public expenditure of 3.6 per cent over four years and a fall in government spending as a proportion of GDP from 47.3 per cent to 40.9 per cent for 2014/15, given the growth forecast for that period.[3]

---

2   HMT (2010: Table C13, p. 102).

3   HMT (2010)

Table 11 Overall total managed expenditure plans versus outcomes

	Nominal (£ billion)			Real (2015/16 £ billion)		
	2010/11	2014/15	Change	2010/11	2014/15	Change
Plan	696.8	737.5	5.8%	786.0	757.4	–3.6%
Outturn	714.0	746.7	4.6%	763.7	747.3	–2.1%
	% of GDP					
	2010/11	2014/15				
Plan	47.3	40.9				
Outturn	45.3	40.8				

Source: HMT (2010), including projected GDP deflator series; OBR (2016); ONS (2016).

However, things did not turn out as planned. Table 11 provides a comparison of planned spending changes in nominal and real terms and as a proportion of GDP, for the last parliament, with actual outturns.

Government spending as a proportion of GDP is calculated using market prices which, as has been explained, tends to artificially reduce the government spending ratio.

A number of things become clear when one compares plans with outturns. Firstly, once the upward revision to nominal spending in the year 2010/11 is taken into account, the actual growth in nominal spending between 2010/11 and 2014/15 was lower than expected at 4.6 per cent. However, given the inaccuracy of forecasts for inflation in 2010/11 (inflation being lower over the parliament than expected), the real cut in spending over the period to 2014/15 was lower at 2.1 per cent than the 3.6 per cent cut envisaged by the Chancellor in the July 2010 Budget. In other words, real spending was cut less than planned.

It is well documented that GDP growth (both real and nominal) was significantly lower over the last parliament than expected. It therefore might be surprising to see that the outturn for government spending as a proportion of GDP in 2014/15 was very similar to that which the government had planned in 2010/11 for that year.

This paradoxical result is a statistical rather than a real phenomenon. In Q2 2014 there was a change in the way GDP was measured which was then backdated across the whole period (as discussed in earlier chapters). This caused an upward shift in measured GDP across the whole period. At times this shift was between 5 and 7 per cent.[4] Of course, actual national income was not higher; it is just that the measurement conventions changed. This explains why the outturn for spending as a proportion of GDP was lower in 2010/11 than the planned level – measured GDP was revised upwards. What is important in looking at the extent of spending 'reductions' is that the fall in spending as a proportion of GDP was significantly less than planned when compared on a like-for-like basis. This was partly as a result of cuts in real spending being less than planned and partly as a result of lower than expected growth in GDP.

Despite the impression the media have given, over the last parliament real cuts to government spending were very modest at just 2.1 per cent over the whole period from 2010/11 to 2014/15.

Real spending per capita

While, ultimately, the headline amounts of spending are important in considering the long-term effective tax burden on the UK population, these headline figures can sometimes be misleading.

For example, over the period 2010/11 to 2014/15, there was significant population growth in the UK. Real spending per capita has therefore fallen proportionately to a much greater extent than overall spending. Table 12 outlines this clearly. It shows that real total managed expenditure (TME) per capita has fallen from

---

4   To see this clearly, one can observe the ONS's GDP Revisions Triangles and Real Time Database (http://www.ons.gov.uk/ons/guide-method/method-quality/specific/ec onomy/national-accounts/gdp-revisions-triangles-and-real-time-database/real -time-database-for-gross-domestic-product-at-market-prices--current-prices.xls) and how the figures change in Q2 2014.

Table 12 Real spending per capita (2015/16 prices), 2010/11 to 2014/15

	2010/11	2011/12	2012/13	2013/14	2014/15
Real spending (£ billion)	764	755	744	747	747
Change in real spending since 2010/11		–1.2%	–2.5%	–2.2%	–2.1%
Real spending per capita (£)	12,168	11,923	11,682	11,654	11,569
Change in real spending per capita since 2010/11		–2.0%	–4.0%	–4.2%	–4.9%

Source: OBR (2016), ONS (2016).

£12,168 per person in 2010/11 to £11,569 per person in 2014/15 (a fall of 4.9 per cent).

Composition of spending cuts: types of spending, functions and departments

It is useful to drill down into the composition of spending. When the government sets out its spending plans, it splits spending into two broad types: annually managed expenditure (AME) and departmental expenditure limits (DEL). DELs are spending limits for departments that tend to relate to public services, with the headline figures determined in spending reviews. AME incorporates other types of spending such as debt interest payments, social security payments and other spending areas which tend to fluctuate more broadly. The term 'managed' for this type of expenditure can be confusing because many of the components cannot easily be managed in the short term.

These two components of spending saw very different trends over the course of the last parliament, as shown in Table 13. AME (around 60 per cent of which is made up of social security spending) actually increased by 6.5 per cent in real terms. Departmental spending, on the other hand, was cut by 10.2 per cent in real terms.

Table 13 Government spending 2010/11 to 2014/15

	£ billion, 2015/16 prices		Average annual real growth	Cumulative real growth
	2010/11	2014/15	2010/11 to 2014/15	
Total managed expenditure	£763.7	£747.3	–0.5%	–2.1%
AME	£367.8	£391.7	1.6%	6.5%
DEL	£395.8	£355.5	–2.6%	–10.2%

Source: author's calculations from OBR (2016), ONS (2016).

These figures are made somewhat more complicated by the fact that there have been various redefinitions of types of expenditure between DEL and AME over this period. To compare the figures accurately over time, numerous adjustments have to be made (as outlined by Crawford and Keynes (2015)). For the purposes of this chapter though, which is concerned with the path of overall spending, these changes in distinctions are not particularly important. The raw figures highlight the main story – departmental expenditure has fallen fairly significantly as spending on annual managed expenditure has risen.

To show more clearly how the components of spending evolved over the last parliament, one can examine data on government spending 'by function' from the Public Expenditure Statistical Analyses (HMT 2016a). Splitting spending into broad functions is probably the most economically meaningful classification of government activity, given that many departments contain activities that span more than one broad area. Most obviously, the Department for Business, Innovation and Skills has, for example, been responsible for 'higher education', which falls under the 'education' function of government. Figure 10 examines what has happened to spending in each of the major functions of government since 2010/11.

As can be seen, different 'functions' of government have fared very differently in terms of how spending evolved. International

Figure 10 Real changes in government spending by function 2010/11 to 2014/15

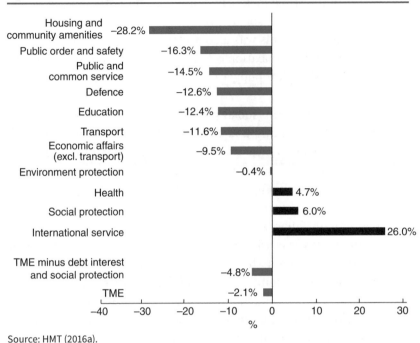

Source: HMT (2016a).

services (26 per cent), health (4.7 per cent) and social protection (6.0 per cent) all saw real terms increases in expenditure. Other functions of government saw significant real-terms cuts. Housing and community amenities (28.2 per cent), public order and safety (16.3 per cent) and, perhaps more surprisingly, education (12.4 per cent) were all functions of government which saw significant overall reductions.

These are largely a reflection of a deliberate prioritisation of spending determined by government policy as outlined in the Spending Reviews of 2010 and 2013. The coalition government pledged to increase spending in real terms on the NHS, to increase spending significantly on international development aid and to institute significant increases in the state pension as a result of its 'triple-lock' (the state pension is the largest single component of the social protection budget). Non-investment spending on schools was also protected, but the changes to the way that higher education is financed and the significant cuts to the schools' capital budget meant that overall education spending fell.

The fact that the social protection budget has seen such an increase in spending and that it is the single largest function of government as measured by spending inevitably means that other areas of government spending have faced greater restraint. To see this, stripping out debt interest and social protection spending from overall expenditure shows that residual spending has actually fallen by 4.8 per cent in real terms.

In other words, the ring-fencing of large areas of government activity has meant that some major functions of government have faced very significant real spending cuts even though cuts overall have been much lower than widely reported. This is the result of a deliberate policy decision by the government. What is perhaps especially interesting is that the long-term trend noted in earlier chapters has continued. Spending on the night watchman functions of the state and spending on capital items has decreased, whereas spending on certain welfare items has increased. In other words, there has been a move towards the more damaging areas of government spending and away from those that are most likely to increase growth.

Although measuring government spending by function gives a more representative picture than comparing departments, we can also see how spending changes have been far from uniform by showing spending broken down into government departments (Figure 11).

The Department for Communities and Local Government has faced the tightest settlement with its Local Government budget (grants to local authorities) falling by 47.5 per cent in real terms and its Communities budget falling by 41.7 per cent. Local

Figure 11 Real changes in DEL by government department 2010/11 to 2014/15

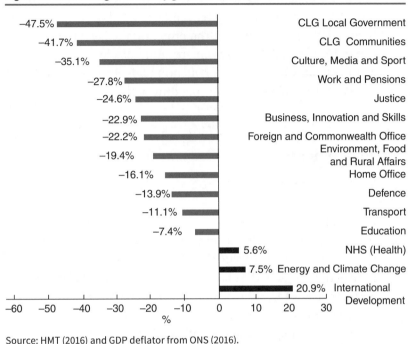

Source: HMT (2016) and GDP deflator from ONS (2016).

authorities, as they have other sources of revenue, have not seen spending cut to this extent, but have faced relatively tough settlements. Other departments have all made fairly significant savings (with the exception of the departments for Health, Energy and Climate Change and International Development), though focusing on DEL spending of course ignores the huge social protection spending budget outlined above.

As Crawford and Keynes (2015) outlined, not all of these changes in government departmental spending were as anticipated from the 2010 spending review. Since then the Departments of Health, Education, Business, Innovation and Skills, and Transport have benefited from unexpectedly low inflation or a loosening of spending whereas the Home Office and the Ministry of Justice have faced tighter than expected outturns. But the broad picture has been that the protection of certain areas and expanding of social protection spending has led to quite significant restraint in some departmental budgets and a significant redistribution of government spending between functions.

Government spending under the Conservative government

Overall spending and the Spending Review

The Conservative Party won the general election promising to restrain government spending further. This included a promise to deliver a budget surplus by the end of the parliament. At the time of the election, the chancellor George Osborne claimed that no further net tax rises would be necessary to close the deficit and that the remainder of discretionary deficit reduction would occur through spending cuts alone. Following the election victory, the July 2015 budget announced the scope for a 'Spending Review', to be published alongside the 2015 Autumn Statement, which would detail where savings would be made from government departments.

As in the previous parliament, the scope of this review of expenditure was far from comprehensive. Given the growth and tax revenue forecasts, as well as the expected path of interest rates and debt interest payments, the government estimated that £37 billion of fiscal consolidation was necessary over the course of the parliament to deliver their planned surplus. The July 2015 budget set out how to achieve £17 billion of that sum by 2019/20 (£12 billion by 2019/20 from the working-age welfare budget and £5 billion by 2019/20 from clamping down on tax avoidance and evasion). The remainder of the savings would need to be found from reductions to departmental expenditure – the subject of the spending review. But this talk of 'cuts' always masked the fact that, in real terms, overall government spending was planned to remain fairly constant overall between 2015/16 and 2019/20. Once again, however, different functions were to be treated very differently.

As in the previous parliament, the effective ring-fencing (both explicit and implicit) of the vast majority of government expenditure means that any planned spending restraint is heavily concentrated in a limited number of areas. Not only is all pensioner spending effectively exempt from cuts, but, in departmental terms, the government committed to increasing English NHS funding by £10 billion by 2020/21, to raising the Ministry of Defence budget by 0.5 per cent a year in real terms, to spending 0.7 per cent of the UK's gross national income on overseas development aid, and to protecting per pupil schools funding in real terms.

As it happens, when the Autumn Statement and Spending Review were delivered, the government announced that OBR revisions to tax revenue forecasts and lower-than-previously-expected forecasts for debt interest payments over this parliament had led to a forecast structural £27 billion improvement in the public finances. In response, the government did not decide to reduce the deficit more quickly than planned, but, instead, to alleviate some of the planned spending cuts (such as the planned cuts to tax credits and to the police budget). The government also raised taxes, meaning that future spending levels are now forecast to be much higher than originally planned back in July 2015.

The 2016 March Budget showed a significant deterioration in the government's finances. In reaction, the Chancellor of the Exchequer proposed some further cuts to departmental expenditure for much later in the parliament, which as yet are unspecified. It would be reasonable to suppose that he was hoping that they would never have to be implemented, perhaps if economic growth turned out higher than expected.

Table 14 Comparison of real government spending forecasts from July Budget 2015, November Autumn Statement 2015 and March Budget 2016 (2015/16 prices)

		2015/16	2019/20	Change
July Budget 2015				
	TME	742.3	746.8	0.6%
	DEL	351.4	339.0	−3.5%
	AME	390.9	407.8	4.3%
Autumn Statement 2015				
	TME	755.7	762.2	0.9%
	DEL	351.5	346.2	−1.5%
	AME	404.2	416.0	2.9%
March Budget 2016				
	TME	753.9	753.9	0.0%
	DEL	352.1	344.5	−2.2%
	AME	401.9	409.4	1.9%

Source: OBR (2016).

These developments are shown in Table 14. Overall spending is projected to be higher throughout the period now than it was forecast to be in July 2015 in real terms. But expenditure between 2015/16 and 2019/20 is expected to be broadly flat. Within the total, AME expenditure will rise by much less than planned (not least due to the downward revision in debt interest payments), but the planned real-terms cuts to departmental expenditure have also been reduced overall since the first budget after the election. Real-terms departmental expenditure is now planned to fall by just 2.2 per cent over the course of this parliament, rather than the 3.5 per cent planned in July 2015.

Since the Budget, we have of course had the unexpected referendum result in favour of UK exit from the European Union. It is widely acknowledged that this is likely to depress economic activity somewhat relative to the expectations on which the forecasts were based that were used to determine the 2016 Budget's spending totals. Already, the new Chancellor of the Exchequer, Philip Hammond, has said that the government will relax plans to achieve a budget surplus by 2020 – though it is unclear whether this reflects an expectation of an economic slowdown over that period (and thus higher spending and lower tax revenues) or whether the government is set to increase discretionary spending. Either way, it seems that spending by the end of this parliament is likely to be higher than outlined above, so that overall real spending will probably rise over this parliament.

Departmental expenditure

The government has set out departmental expenditure plans in its most recent spending review, which allows us to examine the planned changes to real-terms spending by department between 2015/16 and 2019/20. This process is made somewhat more complicated by the fact the new prime minister, Theresa May, has recently reconfigured departments, including abolishing the Department for Energy and Climate Change and rolling its functions into a new department combining it with many of the functions of the old Department for Business, Innovation and Skills. Two other new departments, one for leaving the European Union and another for international trade, have also been established. At the forthcoming Autumn Statement we are expecting the government to update its projections for departmental spending to account for these developments. To get an idea of the broad trends prior to these changes, however, Figure 12 presents projected departmental spending from the most recent Public Expenditure Statistical Analyses based on the old department structure.

This breakdown reflects the political priorities outlined above. With the exception of transport, the other departments which will see projected increases in real spending or minor cuts to real spending are those where major areas of activity within the department have been protected. Local government funding from

Figure 12 Real changes in DEL by government department 2015/16 to 2019/20

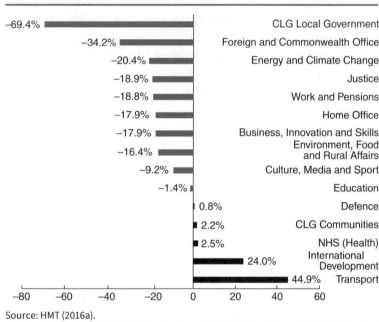

Source: HMT (2016a).

central government will be cut hard, but this partly reflects the large transfer of business rate revenue collection to local authorities. But other departments, such as Business, Innovation and Skills (17.9 per cent), Culture, Media and Sport (9.2 per cent) and Justice (18.9 per cent) will see large cuts to their budgets, though these three departments accounted for just 3.3 per cent of overall government spending in 2015/16.

The reckoning up: government spending 2010/11 to 2019/20

Given that the Conservative Party has been in government for the last two parliaments, and its political priorities in terms

Figure 13 Nominal and real expenditure (£ billion; real expenditure in 2015/16 prices) and spending as a proportion of GDP

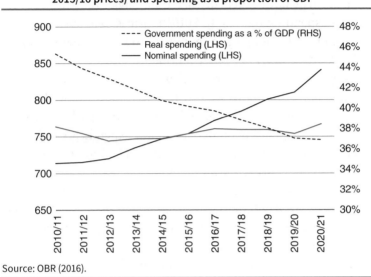

Source: OBR (2016).

of spending have been largely constant across that period, it is worth reflecting on what has happened to spending across the whole period between 2010/11 and 2014/15 combined with the projections through to 2019/20.

On the latest projections, overall government spending will have risen in nominal terms from £714.0 billion in 2010/11 to £810.4 billion in 2019/20. In real terms this reflects a cut in overall expenditure of just 1.3 per cent – from £763.7 billion to £753.9 billion in 2015/16 prices. Given the forecasts for growth in the 2016 Budget (which, it must be said, are highly uncertain), this would mean that total government expenditure as a proportion of GDP will have fallen from 45.3 per cent in 2010/11 to 37.0 per cent by 2019/20 (see Figure 13). As noted above, the spending ratios as a proportion of national income at factor cost would be of the order of five percentage points higher.

Given population growth over the period, real spending per head will have fallen further than suggested through the headline spending figures. In 2015/16 prices, real spending will fall from £12,168 per person in 2010/11 to £11,264 per person in 2019/20, a drop of 7.4 per cent over that period.

As was noted before, however, examining headline total government spending figures hides information on how the composition of spending has changed. Over the two parliaments, for example, real spending on departmental expenditure will have fallen from £395.8 billion in 2010/11 to £344.5 billion in 2019/20 (a cut of 13 per cent), while annual managed expenditure, which includes debt interest payments and the state pension, will have risen from £367.8 billion to £409.4 billion (an increase of 11.3 per cent). In other words, the small overall cut to expenditure masks large changes to spending on particular activities.

Of course, all of these forward-looking projections of spending are subject to change. But evidence from the last parliament suggests that, by and large, Spending Review decisions tend to stick. Between the election and the Spending Review, however, projected government spending has increased above the originally expected levels. This higher spending is expected to be financed initially by higher tax revenues and lower debt interest payments. However, now that the forecasts have worsened, there are projected to be further increases in taxation and some as-yet unspecified cuts to departmental budgets.

Despite all the talk of austerity and spending cuts, we can draw some important overall conclusions. Real spending is only expected to have fallen very slightly over the period 2010/11 to 2019/20. But, significant forecast GDP growth over the decade means that, as a proportion of GDP, the overall size of the state measured by government spending will have fallen substantially (if the forecasts prove correct), though to still high levels. Government spending will be approximately the same proportion of GDP at market prices as it was in 2000 and five percentage points higher than in 1960. However, the overall spending totals mask a significant increase in spending in some areas, not least social protection, while departmental expenditure has been cut significantly. Even within departmental spending, significant ring-fencing of certain budgets (often undertaken for political reasons) has meant that some departments have seen very deep cuts while others have been insulated from restraint.

ANNEX TO CHAPTER 4

David B. Smith

A misleading political myth in the austerity debate

The political debate ahead of the May 2015 general election featured some serious misrepresentations concerning the subject of this chapter, which were never properly exposed at the time. One such myth was that Mr Osborne's December 2014 Autumn Statement implied that the Chancellor was planning to cut government spending back to the level of the 1930s. This claim was a pure canard (Smith 2015).

The Road to Wigan Pier?

In fact, Table 9 reveals that the aggregate spending ratio was 33.1 per cent of factor-cost GDP in 1938, well below the 46.4 per cent recorded in 2014. The subsequent methodological changes to the data, discussed earlier, mean that old Autumn Statement projections need to be handled with caution. However, Mr Osborne's plans set out in the December 2014 Autumn Statement envisaged a general government spending ratio of 39.8 per cent of factor-cost GDP by 2019/20 using the definitions of the time. This would have represented the lowest ratio since 1964, not 1938, and was only some 1 per cent below Labour's 'prudence' era spending in 2000. In the event, the target for 2019/20 was revised up to 41.1 per cent in the 2015 Autumn Statement, and to 41.9 per cent in the March 2016 Budget, although both of these figures were

Figure 14 Ratio of UK government 'primary' expenditure (i.e. excluding
debt interest) to UK GDP at factor cost 1870–2015

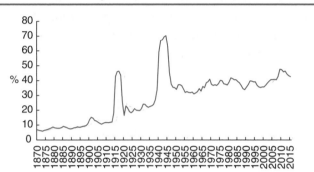

calculated using different accounting conventions. However, it
would take a brave individual to bet that even the March 2016
Budget figures will not be further overshot, given subsequent
political events.

In addition, the composition of government spending was
quite different in the 1930s. A far higher share was going on debt
interest payments, which had peaked at 9.6 per cent of GDP in
1926 and were still 6 per cent in 1938 (see Figure 9). So-called 'primary' spending – i.e. total spending less debt interest – averaged
21.6 per cent of factor-cost GDP between 1920 and 1938, compared with 45% since 2010 and 39.8 per cent under the 1997–2010
Labour government (Figure 14). The other special factor in the
1930s was the increased expenditure on defence in the run up
to World War II. Defence spending had increased from some
2.6 per cent of factor-cost GDP in the early 1930s to 6.8 per cent
by 1938, compared with the 2 per cent now being targeted by the
present government. Spending on non-defence and non-debt interest was around 20.3 per cent of factor-cost GDP in 1938 compared with the 34.1 per cent of GDP projected for such items in
2019/20 in the 2014 Autumn Statement. In other words, the sort

of public services on which the left likes to see money spent (the non-nightwatchmen functions of the state) was 13.8 percentage points more – or 1.7 times as much – as a proportion of GDP in the 2014 Autumn Statement projection for 2019/20 than was being spent just before World War II.

5 SPENDING, TAX AND ECONOMIC WELFARE

David B. Smith

Government expenditure by function

In contrast to Table 3, which focuses on the national accounts definitions of government spending and taxation, Table 15 uses the presentation preferred by HM Treasury for monitoring and control purposes, as set out in the March 2016 Budget for fiscal year 2016/17. This presentation provides more detail on individual spending programmes and tax revenues. However, it also includes public corporations, unlike the general government definition of government spending used until now. It was the Total Managed Expenditure (TME) measure which was involved in the BBC's claim that Mr Osborne was planning to take the government spending ratio back to the 1930s. Rather belatedly, this claim was officially disproved in Chart 4.14 of the OBR's July 2015 Summer Budget report. However, as we have shown, the claim was based in any case on the misunderstanding of the government spending ratio.

On the receipts side, a striking feature of Table 15 is the contribution made by income tax and national insurance to the government's revenues: they have a joint contribution of almost 42.4 per cent. However, VAT still delivers a substantial 19.8 per cent of receipts, with excise duties providing another 7 per cent. This does not mean that other taxes that raise less revenue cannot have deleterious second-round effects on activity and employment, however, if marginal rates are high or the tax bears little relation to the ability to pay.

Table 15   March 2016 Budget forecasts for UK public spending by function and government receipts in 2016/17

	Total spending on function £bn	% of total managed expenditure/ receipts	Ratio to GDP at market prices (%)	Ratio to GDP at factor cost (%)
Total Managed Expenditure (TME)				
Social protection	240	31.1	12.4	14.1
Personal social services	30	3.9	1.5	1.8
Health	145	18.8	7.5	8.5
Transport	29	3.8	1.5	1.7
Education	102	13.2	5.3	6.0
Defence	46	6.0	2.4	2.7
Debt interest	39	5.1	2.0	2.3
Industry, agriculture and employment	24	3.1	1.2	1.4
Public order and safety	34	4.4	1.8	2.0
Housing and environment	34	4.4	1.8	2.0
Other	49	6.3	2.5	2.9
TME	772	100	39.7	45.3
Government receipts				
Income tax	182	25.5	9.4	10.7
National insurance	126	17.6	6.5	7.4
Excise duties	48	6.7	2.5	2.8
Corporation tax	43	6.0	2.2	2.5
VAT	138	19.3	7.1	8.1
Business rates	28	3.9	1.4	1.6
Council tax	30	4.2	1.5	1.8
Other (taxes)	69	9.7	3.6	4.0
Other (non-taxes)	51	7.1	2.6	3.0
Total receipts	715	100	36.8	41.9

Source: HM Treasury Budget 2016, 16 March 2016, Pie Charts 1 and 2, pp. 5–6. Unlike in Table 9, this table uses the published Budget forecasts for money GDP, not rescaled figures to allow for the amendments published in June 2016.

Looking at the expenditure side, Table 15 reveals that only 10.4 per cent of government expenditure is accounted for by the two 'primary' government functions of external defence and the maintenance of law and order. Even adding in debt interest only brings that total to 15.5 per cent of government spending or 7 per cent of factor-cost GDP. This contrasts with the three big items of social protection (14.1 per cent of factor-cost GDP), health (8.5 per cent) and education (6 per cent).

Divergent consequences of the different forms of government spending

Both the macroeconomic and microeconomic consequences of different types of government expenditure differ from each other. The international growth literature (OECD 2003) suggests that public investment in infrastructure, such as transport links or primary and secondary education, can add to a country's growth potential, and are known as 'productive expenditures'. However, these should only be undertaken if the marginal rate of return exceeds the opportunity cost of allocating the same resources elsewhere, including to output-stimulating tax cuts.[1]

However, increased governmental consumption appears to reduce national output. This is likely to be because the resources diverted to supply such expenditures would be better employed in the private sector. In particular, the evidence from international cross-section and panel-data studies suggests that almost all increases in the share of governmental expenditure in GDP lead to a near one-for-one reduction in the share allocated to private

---

1 This is why political vanity projects such as the HS2 rail link should not be undertaken, even if they are treated as an investment in the national accounts. HS2 may raise growth (very slightly in aggregate terms), but the additional benefits from growth are unlikely to be greater than the costs – in other words, spending the money elsewhere (or not taking it away in taxation) would have been likely to add more value to the economy.

capital formation. This under-capitalisation takes the economy onto a lower, but parallel, growth path according to 'neo-classical' growth models but leads to an additional permanent reduction in the growth rate in the context of a 'post-neo-classical endogenous-growth' model (see Sinclair (2012: 82–84) for a tabular summary of the empirical research since 1975).

Transfer payments are likely to reduce economic growth in various ways, not least because of the supply-side effects of the taxes necessary to finance them. Unlike with government investment, there is unlikely to be any offsetting effect on growth. These have grown rapidly over the last century (see Figure 15). Transfers in the form of pensions and other payments to people at older ages are likely to reduce saving in the private sector and fixed capital formation. However, the most potentially counter-productive public expenditure appears to be paying means-tested welfare benefits to the population of working age. These reduce potential GDP because of their impact in reducing the supply of labour to the private sector, which exacerbates the effect of the taxes necessary to finance them.

Of course, some welfare schemes are better designed than others. For example, one of the intentions behind in-work tax credits (which will evolve into universal credit) was to increase the supply of labour by encouraging people to undertake low-paid employment rather than solely relying on state benefits. It has had that effect, but it also seems to have encouraged people to undertake the bare minimum of work required to qualify for tax credits (16 hours) but then not to climb the ladder of opportunity by taking on additional hours or extra responsibilities. The average part-time employee worked for 16.1 hours in February/April 2016, according to the ONS Labour Market Statistics for June 2016. This is not surprising given the very high withdrawal rates for tax credits as earnings increase. However, it is debatable whether tax credits have raised the total number of hours worked in the British economy (and, hence, national output), or reduced them.

Figure 15 Ratios of welfare payments and social security taxes to UK GDP at factor cost 1900–2015

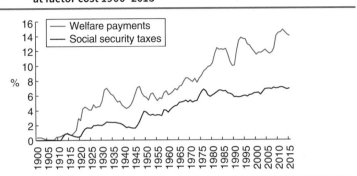

The OECD has suggested that only around one fifth of government spending falls into the 'productive' category. This means that most other expenditure items are 'non-productive' and may be primarily intended to 'bribe' voters (that is, finance transfers or services that are desired by particular voter groups), buy off vested interest groups or, in some countries, reward political cronies, along the lines suggested by public choice theory.[2]

Just as transfer payments have risen, government investment has fallen as a percentage of GDP (despite the rise in overall expenditure). Again, public choice considerations may explain this as the benefits of investment spending are longer term whereas the costs are short term (see Figure 16).

In summary, there has been a big increase in government spending over the last 100 years. However, within the government spending envelope, there has been a particularly large increase in those items that damage the economy most while those items that tend to have a beneficial effect on growth or which damage the economy least have been reduced.

---

2   The public choice literature is discussed in Tullock et al. (2000).

Figure 16 Ratio of UK general government investment to UK GDP at factor cost 1946–2015

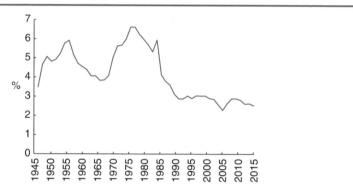

Economic growth and the financing of government spending

When it comes to the impact of how government spending is financed on growth, perhaps the main macroeconomic distinction is that between increases in indirect taxes, where the first-round impact is likely to be inflationary and direct taxes which have fewer initial inflationary consequences but can lead to a withdrawal of labour supply that may be voluntary (for example, income tax) or involuntary (for example, increased employers' national insurance contributions that price people out of work). Ultimately, however, a rise in indirect taxes will raise the price level (thus reducing real wages and leading to an impact on labour supply) if the central bank is willing to tolerate this development. It is possible that a central bank that is following an inflation target may respond to the rise in the price level caused by a rise in indirect taxes by tightening monetary policy. The long-run effects must be the same in the end and will involve a squeeze on real wages while the price level moves in accordance with expectations.

In the long run, when it is the post-tax real incentives to supply goods and services that dominate the decisions of private economic agents, it is likely that the effects of any flat-rate tax hike will tend to have similar results from a macroeconomic perspective. However, increases in indirect taxes are less likely to affect saving detrimentally than increases in direct taxes, because indirect taxes are only charged on consumption and are thus not charged on that part of income that is saved.

More generally, the author has previously reported statistical evidence that suggests that the negative effects of higher taxes and budget deficits on private activity are identical in the long run and quite similar in the short term (see Sinclair 2012: 108–11). This confirms that the primary issue is the size of state spending compared with national output and that the choice between tax and bond finance is a secondary consideration. Ultimately, government spending is financed either by taxes levied now or deferred taxes. If it is financed by borrowing – or deferred taxation – there are supply-side effects of government borrowing crowding out private sector activity as a result of pressures on capital markets or the inflow of capital from overseas raising the exchange rate. Furthermore, consumers might reduce expenditure in anticipation of a higher tax burden in the future.[3]

As far as microeconomic considerations are concerned, there is a long-established public finance literature which examines the consequences of taxation and remains intellectually valid (see Smith (2006) and Sinclair (2012), for example, as well as the discussion later in this book). Unfortunately, it also tends to be largely ignored by politicians who, public choice considerations suggest, want to maximise their share of the vote in marginal

---

3 The possibility that the government might renege on its debt or inflate debt away does not change the argument: it simply imposes the burden on a different group of people.

seats and not general economic welfare. This perhaps explains why the UK has such a long and complex tax code.[4] In fact, the microeconomic effects of tax structure are extremely important. High marginal rates of tax can be extremely damaging to hours worked, enterprise and risk taking, capital formation and the supply of goods and services (see later chapters), as well as being unjust to the individual taxpayers concerned. Furthermore, distortions in the tax system whereby some activities are taxed more than others can be very damaging (again see below and Chapter 1).

The size of government: maximising growth and welfare

Given the macro- and microeconomic effects of government spending and taxation on growth and welfare, as well as the fact that the provision of certain public goods can be regarded as welfare enhancing, it is reasonable to ask whether there are 'growth-maximising' or 'welfare-maximising' levels of government expenditure. There is a third statistic of interest, which is the revenue-maximising level of taxation and spending – if the government is spending beyond this level, it means that a reduction in tax rates will increase growth sufficiently that tax revenues will increase. A government spending beyond this level is totally destructive of economic welfare.

Clearly, there are growth and welfare maximising levels of government spending in theory, but, in practice, it is much more difficult to identify those levels. Indeed, the growth-maximising and welfare-maximising levels of government spending will

---

4 There are so many examples of tax measures that have been introduced for political rather than economic reasons, even since 2010, that an exhaustive list would be impossible. However, an obvious example is the additional tax on buy-to-let landlords (both additional stamp duty and also the limitation of the deductibility for tax purposes of interest costs).

depend on a number of time- and context-specific factors (for example, how mobile labour and capital are – if they are more mobile, tax is more likely to be damaging to growth; how efficiently government provides services; and the shape of the tax system).[5] Despite the practical difficulties, we can make some generalisations and, during this debate, certain rules of thumb – that were based on older national accounts definitions, however – have tended to become accepted by people who have worked in this area (Smith 2006). These included:

- The growth-maximising share of government spending in GDP was some 20–25 per cent of GDP. This was based on the fact that ratios in this range were typical of the fast growing South East Asian 'Tiger' economies, countries such as Japan and Korea in their high growth phases, and even Australia, Canada and Spain in the 1950s. *This indicative range should probably be revised down to some 18.5–23.5 per cent, using current (June 2016) UK definitions.*

- The welfare-maximising share of government spending in GDP[6] was less than some 30–35 per cent of GDP. This conclusion was based on the work of Tanzi and Schuknecht (2000) and Tanzi (2008), who examined the effects of state spending on a range of objective measures of human wellbeing. They concluded that there was no sign of improved outcomes for welfare measures once spending had exceeded these limits.[7] *Subsequent methodological changes*

---

5 There will be more discussion of tax and growth in later chapters.

6 The social welfare maximising point can be defined as the share of national output at which the discounted net present value of the diminishing marginal social utility derived from extra government spending equals the rising opportunity cost in terms of the net present value of the foregone economic output, and also personal liberty, of the need to pay for it.

7 If this seems rather low to modern eyes, almost all the countries summarised in Table 7 were in this range in 1960, as are contemporary Switzerland and Korea, the 'Greater South East' of England, and Britain overall in the mid 1950s. In almost every

to the data suggest that 26.5–32.5 per cent would be the corresponding range in today's terms.

- The upper limit on taxable capacity was around 38 per cent, implying that the public finances eventually became unsustainable if general government expenditure was allowed to increase much beyond 40 per cent of GDP.[8] *On current definitions, the upper limit on taxable capacity in Britain seems to be around 37.5 per cent of factor-cost GDP (Figure 1), or 33 per cent on the market-price measure, suggesting that spending only becomes sustainable when it falls into the 37–38 per cent range.*

The ratios calculated using the factor-cost measure of national income would be higher. However, it is not difficult to convert from one basis to another, using the GDP figures in Table 4. It is also worth noting that Mr Osborne's March 2016 Budget target that government spending should be down to 37.2 per cent of market-price GDP by 2020/21 looks at the upper margin of what is reasonable if the aim is long-term fiscal sustainability, but not, of course, if the aim is welfare maximisation. Certainly, there seems little scope for the new Chancellor, Mr Hammond, to relax his predecessor's spending targets.

---

case, the economic performance of the countries involved would be regarded as highly satisfactory by current (post-2008) standards.

8 It might be asked why the maximum level of government spending is not 33 per cent of national income. Firstly, the British government possesses non-tax incomes of some 2–3 per cent of national output. Also, assuming that the definition of government spending includes debt interest, it could, arguably, run a permanent budget deficit of, say, 1 or 2 per cent of GDP without adverse consequences. Given that overruns of government spending as a proportion of national income in bad times tend to be bigger than undershoots, the government should be operating well within the 37–38 per cent constraint in normal times. Though, as noted above, governments should not seek simply to operate at the point of maximum taxable capacity in any case, as this will be above the welfare-maximising level of taxation.

Conclusions

Because government has almost no resources of its own, all government expenditure usually implies higher taxes either in the present or in the future. Thus, when measuring the burden of government on the private sector, we should look at government spending (rather than taxation) and its relationship with national income.

Measurement of the ratio of government spending to national income is fiendishly difficult. There are several reasons for this, just one of which is that there are several different measures of national output. The measure chosen can make a difference of 5.5 percentage points, or more, to the calculated spending burden. The most appropriate measure is government spending as a proportion of national income measured at factor cost. Commonly, the generally lower ratio of government spending to GDP measured at market prices measure is used.

There are substantial differences in the shares of government spending and taxes in national income within the thirty-four OECD member countries. There are also huge differences between the UK regions. The under 32 per cent spending ratio in the UK's 'Greater South East' would represent the lowest spending ratio in the OECD, while the North East, Wales and Northern Ireland are all noticeably more heavily socialised than any individual OECD member.

The average share of state spending in the twelve countries for which there is continuous data has risen from just over 10 per cent in the late nineteenth century to around 45 per cent at present. Over the last 100 years, there has been a movement towards those categories of government spending that tend to be more damaging (relatively less investment which can raise economic growth; more provision of government-funded services; and more transfers).

Despite the impression given to the contrary, there has been very little 'austerity' in the UK. Real government spending has decreased slightly since 2010, and there are plans to reduce the proportion of government spending in national income further. However, progress has been painfully slow. The March 2016 Budget forecasts indicate that the ratio of UK government spending to GDP will only just dip inside its sustainable range by 2020/21, even if there is no policy relaxation under the new Chancellor.

This long-term increase in the size of the government sector gives rise to the question of at what point do advocates of higher government spending say enough is enough? Current international spending levels are not only well beyond what might be thought of as the welfare-maximising level of government spending, they are pushing (and may, indeed, be beyond) the capacity of most countries to levy taxation. The upper limit to sustainable government spending is probably around 37–38 per cent of national income as presently defined.

Finally, making a success of Brexit will require a sharp improvement in the microeconomic supply-side flexibility of the UK economy as resources have to be shifted from supplying Continental markets to the wider world outside. This supply-side flexibility is unlikely to be achievable while the government sector is absorbing over 45 per cent of the factor-cost measure of UK GDP and the private sector is hamstrung by an excessive regulatory burden, some (but, by no means, all) of which results from having been part of the European Union. If Mrs May's administration lacks the political stomach for major government spending reforms, then a 1950s R. A. Butler–style 'bonfire of controls', together with ex ante revenue-neutral tax simplification and reform, should be two of the overriding economic aims of the new administration.

REFERENCES

Ball, I. and Pflugrath, G. (2012) Government accounting: making Enron look good. *World Economics* 13(1), January–March.

Barro, R. J. (1974) Are government bonds net wealth? *Journal of Political Economy* 82: 1095–117.

Bastable, C. F. (1917) *Public Finance*, 3rd edn. London: Macmillan.

Booth, P. (2011) *Sharper Axes, Lower Taxes: Big Steps to a Smaller State*. Hobart Paperback 38. London: Institute of Economic Affairs.

Crawford, R. and Keynes, S. (2015) Options for further departmental spending cuts. IFS Green Budget 2015. London: Institute for Fiscal Studies.

Feinstein, C. H. (1972) *National Income Expenditure and Output of the United Kingdom*. Cambridge University Press.

Havrylshyn, O., Meng, X. and Tupy, M. L. (2016) 25 years of reforms in ex-communist countries: fast and extensive reforms led to higher growth and more political freedom. Cato Institute Policy Analysis, no. 795.

Hughes, M. (2016) Impact of changes in the national accounts and economic commentary for quarter 1 (Jan to Mar) 2016. UK Office for National Statistics, National Accounts Articles, 30 June 2016 (www.ons.gov.uk).

Hills, S., Thomas, R. and Dimsdale, N. (2010) The UK recession in context – what do three centuries of data tell us? Bank of England Quarterly Bulletin, 2010 Quarter 4.

HMT (2010) Budget 2010. HC 61.

HMT (2016) Public Expenditure Statistical Analyses 2016. Updated 21 July 2016.

ONS (2016) GDP deflators at market prices, and money GDP: June 2016 (Quarterly National Accounts). London: Office for National Statistics.

OBR (2016) Economic and fiscal outlook. March 2016. London: Office for Budget Responsibility.

OECD (2003) *The Sources of Economic Growth in OECD Countries.* Paris: OECD.

OECD (2015) *Revenue Statistics 1965–2014.* Paris: OECD.

OECD (2016) *OECD Economic Outlook.* Paris: OECD.

Sanandaji, N. (2015) *Scandinavian Unexceptionalism: Culture, Markets and the Failure of Third-Way Socialism.* Readings in Political Economy 1. London: Institute of Economic Affairs.

Sinclair, M. (ed.) (2012) The single income tax: final report of the 2020 Tax Commission. London: Tax Payers' Alliance and Institute of Directors.

Smith, D. B. (2006) *Living with Leviathan: Public Spending, Taxes and Economic Performance.* Hobart Paper 158. London: Institute of Economic Affairs.

Smith, D. B. (2009) *How Should Britain's Government Spending and Tax Burdens be Measured? A Historic Perspective on the 2009 Budget Forecasts.* Discussion Paper 35. London: Institute of Economic Affairs.

Smith, D. B. (2012) Britain in the 1950s: lessons for today. *B & O (Britain and Overseas)* 42, no. 3 (www.ercouncil.org).

Smith, D. B. (2014) The modern Leviathan state, its growth and consequences. In *A U-Turn on the Road to Serfdom* (ed. G. Norquist). Occasional Paper 150. London: Institute of Economic Affairs.

Smith, D. B. (2015) *The UK Government Spending Ratio: Back to the 1930s?* London: Politeia.

Sterne, G. and Bayoumi, T. (1993) Temporary cycles or volatile trends? Economic fluctuations in 21 OECD countries. Bank of England Working Paper Series no. 13.

Tanzi, V. (2008) *Regulating for the New Economic Order: The Good, the Bad, and the Damaging.* London: Politeia.

Tanzi, V. (2011) *Government versus Markets: The Changing Economic Role of the State.* Cambridge University Press.

Tanzi, V. and Schuknecht, L. (2000) *Public Spending in the 20th Century: A Global Perspective.* Cambridge University Press.

Tullock, G., Seldon, A. and Brady, G. L. (2000) *Government: Whose Obedient Servant? A Primer in Public Choice.* London: Institute of Economic Affairs.

Young, A. T. (2013) Why in the world are we all Keynesians again? The flimsy case for stimulus spending. Cato Institute Policy Analysis no. 721.

PART 2

**TAXATION AND GROWTH:
THE EMPIRICAL EVIDENCE**

6 TAX AND GROWTH: THEORIES AND EVIDENCE

Patrick Minford

Introduction

If only one could drink from the elixir of growth, surely many problems would be solved. As a result of growth extra resources can be deployed to deal with any issue in hand. For those concerned about the environmental effects of growth, it is important to realise that growth is ideally defined as net of such effects: so, if these outweigh the extra resources, then that is not growth. Of course, in practice, growth is measured in terms of national income per capita; but we need to bear in mind that if policies creating growth, as measured this way, generate damaging side-effects, then the cost of such effects need to be deducted.

For many years economists have sought to create theories of growth – that is, to understand its causes. Initially, all they could come up with was that generating more of the factors of production that create output (namely, labour and capital) would generate extra output and so growth. This rather obvious process was generally thought of as 'exogenous' (outside our powers to control) given that the amount of labour and capital are respectively the result of net births and saving, both of which seem largely outside the control of policymakers. In any case a higher population may lower (or at least dilute) output per head, which is the measure we care about.

This analysis left us with the role of technology, which could be thought of as the factor of production not directly measured as labour and capital. The effect of technology could be measured via the 'gap' or residual between the measured effect of labour and capital and total output produced. This 'Solow residual', named after Robert Solow, one of the early pioneers of growth theory (Solow 1956), was at first also thought of as exogenous: a sort of manna from heaven that rained down on production, courtesy of natural human ingenuity.[1]

More recently, economists have come up with theories of how this residual's behaviour could be affected by government policies or, more broadly, by man-made institutions. When they posit that the permanent growth rate of a country can be affected by such human intervention, these are known as 'endogenous growth' theories; when they posit that growth can be temporarily affected over a significant period of time, in a 'growth episode' causing a once-for-all leap in a country's output level, they are known as 'semi-endogenous growth' theories.

The economics literature on these theories is now very extensive and some is reviewed in L. Minford (2015a) in detail. One strand concerns the way labour becomes more productive by simply performing tasks repeatedly ('learning by doing'). Such ideas have led some to redefine capital more broadly to include human capital (the knowledge embodied in workers). We can then add in complementarities that lead to increasing returns when each worker is more productive when surrounded by other highly skilled workers. Another strand draws on the public good aspects of 'ideas' which 'spill over' from their inventors to the broader economy. This strand models how firms generate ideas systematically by purposeful, profit-motivated investments in research and development (R&D) when there are full or partial intellectual property rights. Knowledge acquisition can be

---

1 For an intuitive overview of modern growth theory, see Solow (1994).

helped along by 'agglomeration', whereby people engaged in certain activities gather together in the same place and share their insights informally and where production processes of different firms tend to be complementary to each other (the City of London being an obvious example). Another strand emphasises that, as workforces become more educated, the sectors that hire better-educated workers expand, while others contract, this process leading to a rise in economy-wide productivity through 'structural transformation'. A final aspect of the literature stresses that entrepreneurs set up innovative firms which 'disrupt' existing ways of doing business, leading to efficiency gains that cannot be achieved by the R&D of incumbent firms alone.

Among policymakers of developed countries, the Washington Consensus emerged in the 1990s, according to which countries should execute reforms to liberalise markets under the rule of law to create an environment favourable to growth. This consensus is apparently supported by the success of certain countries that have turned to such policies in improving their growth prospects. Examples of successful liberalisation are China under Deng Xiao Ping and India after Rajiv Gandhi broke with the Nehru planning model; while failed states such as parts of the ex–Soviet Union, Cuba and the Sudan provide many examples of the opposite. However, this evidence can be thought of as gathered from uncontrolled policy experiments, where many elements in the economic environment have been varied at the same time and so it is impossible to distinguish the role of each in the experiment. These experiments do tell us that, to avoid disaster, many elements have to change together and that, in achieving success, there are many factors at work. But there are also instances where these policies have been tried in some combination with other policies and have failed in important respects. What we need is further evidence of what the effect is of varying some element to some extent, within a generally successful economy; or, similarly, which reforms should be the first to be 'sequenced' in a generally disastrous economy; or, again, which elements are strictly necessary for success. For this we need somehow to isolate the effects of particular policies.

It is in this context that the chapters in this part of the book will examine the influence of taxation and some regulatory interventions on growth. We know the general conditions that can promote growth and the general conditions that lead to economic failure. We will try to isolate the specific impact of taxation and regulation on economic growth.

There is a considerable amount of empirical microeconomic research on these topics. And there are very good theoretical reasons to assume that taxes and regulation affect growth because they affect the processes discussed above: the incentives to supply labour and capital; the incentives to innovate and adopt new technology; the incentives to ensure that labour and capital are employed efficiently; and so on.

The association between tax and growth: growth regressions

Various macroeconomic empirical studies have examined the different government policies and institutions that contribute to overall growth through one or other of the channels described above. It is at this macroeconomic level that some have suggested that theory is well ahead of empirical work because of the difficulties in assessing in practice which policies work and which do not.

The standard empirical study of growth policies involves what is known as a panel data regression. A panel data set in this case covers many countries' individual behaviour over time – in other words, it is like a combination of time-series and cross-section data. It might involve, for example, thirty countries over twenty years divided into four five-year averages. On the left-hand side of the regression is growth (the variable we are trying to explain). On the right-hand side is a set of control variables, supposed to operate on all countries at all times and which are possible variables that explain growth. Examples of these variables are the rate of investment as a share of GDP (to capture the direct effect of capital on output through the production function); the initial level of output relative to the richest countries (to capture 'catch-up' by the poor countries by simple technology imitation or absorption); and the growth of the labour force (again a direct production input). Then, in addition to these variables, the researcher can add the indicator of the relevant policy being investigated. There have been a large number of such studies and the results suggest that there is a strong association between low taxes and economic growth.

Surveys of growth regressions

An important set of work that became known as the 'Barro growth regressions' has been widely used to investigate policy impacts since Barro (1991). These take the form of a regression of either GDP growth or productivity growth on initial income (to control for convergence or 'catch-up'), some factors to account for other influences, and a variable measuring the policy factor under investigation. Models of this type are often estimated in a panel of cross-country and time-series data with observations averaged over five-year periods to smooth out the impact of the business cycle. Barro (1991) uses data for 98 countries between 1960 and 1985.

There are two surveys, Leach (2003) and OECD (Leibfritz et al. 1997), which document the empirical literature on the effects of taxation on growth and output levels. Table 16 sets out a selection of the major studies, noting their data set, the explanatory variables used and the main effects of tax on growth that are found. All control for various factors other than taxation (usually different variables across different studies). Some of these studies use tax as the explanatory variable and others use government

Table 16   The negative impact of taxation on economic growth

Author	Data coverage	Main explanatory variables	Comment
Barro (1991)	98 countries in the period 1960–85	Human capital, government consumption, political instability indicator, price distortion	1% point increase in tax-to-GDP ratio lowers output per worker by 0.12%
Koester and Kormendi (1989)	63 countries for which at least five years of continuous data exists for the 1970s	Marginal tax rates, average tax rate, mean growth in labour force and population	10% decrease in marginal tax rates would increase per capita income in an average industrial country by more than 7%
Hansson and Henrekson (1994)	Industry-level data for 14 OECD countries	Government transfers, consumption, total outlays; education expenditure; government investment	Government transfers, consumption and total outlays have a negative impact on growth whilst government investment is not significant
Cashin (1995)	23 OECD countries over the 1971–88 period	Ratio of public investment to GDP, ratio of current taxation revenue to GDP, ratio of expenditure on transfers to GDP	1% point increase in tax-to-GDP ratio lowers output per worker by 2%
Engen and Skinner (1996)	US modelling together with a sample of OECD countries	Marginal tax rates, human capital, investment	2.5% point increase in tax-to-GDP ratio reduces GDP growth by 0.2–0.3%
OECD: Leibfritz et al. (1997)	OECD countries over the 1965–95 period	Tax-to-GDP ratio, physical and human capital formation and labour supply	10% point increase in tax-to-GDP ratio reduces GDP growth by 0.5–1.0%

spending. In theory, the latter is preferable because government spending measures the total claim on the economic resources of government.

Barro (1991) does, in fact, consider that some government spending, in theory at least, might have a positive impact on growth. He believes that there may be a positive effect of

Continued

Author	Data coverage	Main explanatory variables	Comment
Alesina et al. (2002)	18 OECD countries over the 1960–96 period	Primary spending, transfers, labour taxes, taxes on business, indirect taxes, government wage consumption (all in share of GDP)	1% increase in government spending relative to GDP lowers the investment-to-GDP ratio of 0.15% and a cumulative fall of 0.74% after five years
Bleaney et al. (2000)	17 OECD countries over the 1970–94 period	Distortionary tax, productive expenditure, net lending, labour force growth, investment ratio	1% point increase in distortionary tax revenue reduces GDP growth by 0.4% points
Folster and Henrekson (2000)	Sample of rich OECD/ non-OECD countries over the 1970–95 period	Tax-to-GDP, government expenditure-to-GDP, investment-to-GDP, labour force growth, human capital growth	10% point increase in tax-to-GDP ratio reduces GDP growth by 1%
Bassanini and Scarpetta (2001)	21 OECD countries over the 1971–98 period	Indicators of government size and financing, physical capital, human capital, population growth	1% point increase in tax-to-GDP ratio reduces per capita output levels by 0.3–0.6%

education spending on human capital formation and therefore on growth and takes that into account. As such, he examines the impact of real government consumption net of spending on both education and defence as a per cent of real GDP over the period 1970–85 on both real economic growth (averaged over the period 1960–85) and on private investment. He finds a negative correlation between net government spending (so defined) and growth.

Koester and Kormendi (1989) examine the effect of measures of the marginal and average tax rates, as well as population and labour force growth on economic growth. In a cross-country analysis for the 1970s, they find a significant negative effect of marginal tax rates on the level of real GDP per capita, but not on the rate of growth when this is controlled for the initial level of income. They suggest that, holding average tax rates constant, a 10 percentage point decrease in marginal tax rates would increase per capita income in an average industrial country by more than 7 per cent (and in an average developing country by more than 15 per cent). Thus, a revenue-neutral tax reform which reduces tax progressivity would raise incomes.

Alesina et al. (2002) focus on the extent of government spending of various sorts on the investment-to-GDP ratio (and hence by implication on growth). They concluded that, via the effect of raising private sector labour costs, a 1 percentage point increase in government spending relative to GDP resulted in a decrease in the investment-to-GDP ratio of 0.15 percentage points and a cumulative fall of 0.74 percentage points after five years.

In general these studies, with their varying methodologies, find that there is a measurable negative effect of higher tax rates on growth. The order of magnitude of this effect is around 0.5–1.0 per cent for a 10 per cent rise in the ratio of taxation (or government spending) to GDP.

The OECD's own conclusion from its survey was that:

> A number of studies, influenced by the new growth theories, have taken a top-down approach to assess the impact of taxes on per capita income and growth at the macro level. Several of them purport to demonstrate a significant negative relationship between the level of the tax/GDP ratio (or the government expenditure ratio) and the growth rate of GDP per capita, implying that high tax rates reduce economic growth ... our estimates [using a top-down cross country regression] suggest that the increase in the average (weighted) tax rate of about 10 percentage points over the past 35 years, may have reduced OECD annual growth rates by about 0.5 percentage points.

The OECD suggests that a 10 percentage point cut in the tax-to-GDP ratio could increase economic growth by 0.5–1.0

percentage points. Thus they also say that 'up to one third of the growth deceleration in the OECD [over the 1965–95 period] would be explained by higher taxes. In some European countries, tax burdens increased much more dramatically than the OECD average, which would imply correspondingly larger effects on their growth rates' (Leibfritz et al. 1997). A summary of a number of the main studies is shown in Table 16.

Later studies show similar associations. For example, Afonso and Furceri (2008)[2] examine a number of EU and other OECD countries over the period 1970–2004. As well as several components of government expenditure and taxation, they include variables such as initial output, population growth, investment ratio, human capital and openness. Their finding is that a 1 percentage point point rise in the government spending to GDP ratio cuts growth in the OECD by 0.12 per cent and in the EU by 0.13 per cent. Larger effects can be found for individual expenditure and tax components with indirect taxes and social contributions appearing to be the most damaging for growth and worse than income tax. Subsidies and government current expenditure have the worst negative effects on growth on the spending side.

Overall, the tax (or government spending) and growth studies, indicate a strong association between the two variables. As a rule of thumb, it would appear that a 10 percentage point fall in the share of national income taken in tax would lead to slightly more than a 1 percentage point increase in the growth rate – results of this order of magnitude occur over and over again.

This does not mean that the UK can automatically expect to increase its growth rate by 1 percentage point if the government reduces the proportion of national income it spends from (say) 45 per cent to (say) 35 per cent. Firstly, there is the issue of causality. For example, does high government spending lead to low growth

---

2 Reported in the Taxpayers' Alliance, Single Income Tax Report: http://2020tax
.org/2020tc.pdf.

Box 3   Problems with traditional growth regressions

The problems with traditional growth regressions will be discussed in Chapter 7. However, it is useful to highlight one or two of the main points from that chapter here.

Association does not demonstrate causality

Although there is clearly a strong association between tax and growth, this does not mean that low taxes cause high growth. It is perhaps easier to illustrate the 'association does not mean causation' problem by looking at a different policy variable – the rule of law.

Suppose a researcher wishes to determine the impact of the rule of law on growth and that the rule of law coefficient is found to be statistically significant and positive. We now come to the question of interpretation. The researcher implicitly believes that this result tests his hypothesis that the rule of law increases growth. However, it could also be the case that growth encourages the rule of law, through a process whereby a more dynamic business environment creates more demand for dispute resolution or leads to pressure on government for better court services. Or it could be that some other process that we cannot directly observe (perhaps culture or history) encourages both growth and the rule of law. This is known as the problem of identification: we do not have any means to identify which theory is at work in the data because several could account for what we observe.

or the other way round? This is discussed in more detail in Box 3. Secondly, the results are averages using data taken from a wide variety of situations. Thirdly, the effects are likely to be non-linear. The impact of a 1 percentage point change in government spending

This set of problems is well known among researchers and policy analysts. Yet it has had little impact on empirical research, which continues to look for such associations as if they do show causation, on the ground that other interpretations are not credible. Unfortunately, theories abound supporting these alternative interpretations. What is more, many of the features of societies that are supposed to enhance their economic growth are features that are found in many wealthy societies all at the same time, making it impossible to distinguish which is causing which.

Other technical problems of growth regressions

There are other problems, discussed in detail later in this book in a wider context that make it difficult to interpret the results of growth regressions. They include:

- Such regressions capture average effects that might not be applicable in particular countries or in particular periods.
- Generally, it is marginal tax rates that affect growth but growth regressions tend to rely on average tax rates because the data are easier to collect and interpret.
- Some types of government spending may improve growth, though others may not. To some extent, therefore, whether increased taxes reduce growth may depend on how the government spends the money (see Part 1).
- Outliers can mean that the results of growth regressions are not applicable to the wider range of countries.

relative to national income cannot simply be multiplied by 10 to find the impact for a 10 percentage point change. Intuitively, it is likely that the gains in terms of extra growth at the margin will reduce as the tax burden falls and rise as the tax burden increases.

Nevertheless, the rule of thumb may be a starting point for discussion and further investigation though there is a need to develop more robust models in this area of economics as is discussed in the next chapter.

Modelling growth, taxation and investment incentives

Some work has been undertaken that goes beyond growth regressions and, instead, tests competing theories against each other. As has been noted, it is not universally accepted that lower taxes and government spending will lead to higher growth. Some argue that higher government spending leads to the provision of investment incentives, research and development, education and various public goods that might be conducive to growth. Indeed, some argue that a larger role for government in the economy might involve more government direction of investment and, if this is successful, higher growth. Such an interventionist, or activist approach, is exemplified by Aghion and Howitt (1998). For them, growth is seen as depending on government subsidies to investment and to research and development specifically.

Work published in Minford and Wang (2011)[3] examines the interventionist versus incentives model. To approximate the investment subsidy the authors took the difference between the world real interest rate and the national real interest rate. While this difference will be cyclical, as the real interest differential and the expected real exchange rate respond to shocks, over the decadal averages used in the modelling, such effects should be minimal, leaving the systematic effect of government policy in protecting industry against world real capital costs. The mechanism by which real interest rates are held down is through government subsidy for investment which increases the capital

---

3   From which this section is adapted.

intensity of an economy (unless it substitutes for private sector investment). This, in turn, reduces the marginal rate of return to capital, which will reduce the national real interest rate below the international real interest rate. While data on subsidies to research and development (R&D) are not readily available, there are data on the amount of government spending on R&D and this is used as a measure of the subsidy to R&D (of course, government R&D spending is not charged for and can be considered 100 per cent subsidised).

The impact of tax on growth is easier to model. Here the relationship between the growth rate of GDP per capita, the tax rate, a dummy variable specific to each time period, and a dummy variable specific to each country is modelled. Panel data were used that were averaged over consecutive decades from 1970 to 2000 for 100 countries. Data on the growth rate in real GDP per capita and tax rate originate from the Penn World Table Version 6.1 (Heston et al. 2002).

Overall, the modelling found an overwhelmingly strong negative relationship between tax and growth, with some models showing a stronger relationship than others. Specifically, in the preferred model there is an elasticity of growth to tax of approximately –1.4 at the mean of the growth rate (1.6 per cent). The effects are not expected to be linear as the tax rate changes, but, if they were, then a fall in the tax rate by 25 per cent of its existing value (from about 40 per cent to about 30 per cent of national income in the UK) would lead to a rise in the growth rate to 2.7 per cent if the initial growth rate were 2 per cent.

This is roughly in line with the growth regression results discussed above – the impact is a little below the 'rule of thumb' of a 1 percentage point increase in growth from a 10 percentage points cut in the tax-to-GDP ratio, but it is of the same order of magnitude.

When the model was tested further, it was found that the basic results are not greatly dependent on initial GDP per capita (which should control for a country's potential to 'catch up': the lower the starting level of GDP, the greater the growth); human capital; physical capital stock; and the ratio of investment to GDP.

In looking at the activist approach, the relationship between the growth rate and government subsidies to investment and to R&D (as defined above) were examined. It was found that there was no statistically significant relationship between R&D and growth. Indeed, insofar as there is any relationship at all, it was a negative relationship between growth and both investment incentives and R&D, which would appear to deny the proposition of Aghion and Howitt (1998) that the growth rate depends positively upon investment and R&D subsidies. It is not, however, the negative relationship but the absence of a positive relationship which is most interesting. Again control variables were added to test for sensitivity, but do not change the results.

These results add to the body of evidence in two ways. Firstly, they provide another test of the idea that taxes affect growth. Secondly, they seem to cast a great deal of doubt on the ability of government intervention of the sort modelled, financed through taxes, to help growth. This is particularly interesting given that the spending being modelled is that form of government spending that is most likely to have a positive effect on growth.

Tax and growth modelling: a new approach

It was to solve the problems with traditional growth regressions that researchers at Cardiff University built an alternative testing procedure for theories of growth. A model of the UK economy was built in which growth depends on tax and regulation policy (L. Minford 2015b). In order to provide an up-to-date summary of the empirical work on taxation and growth, the model is described and the results are briefly reported here. They are discussed in much greater detail in Chapters 7 and 8.

The model was simulated many times to generate parallel samples of how history could have turned out. An approach known as 'indirect inference' was used which was originally proposed as a method for estimating non-linear macroeconomic models by Tony Smith (1993). This procedure has a remarkably high power to reject false models, because false models generally simulate quite different sorts of behaviour from each other in the face of shocks.[4] If the model effectively replicates history, then there is a high probability that the model represents reality well. Traditional modelling techniques, on the other hand, can come close to 'data-mining' (in other words, the computer can find a good fit to various, not necessarily correct, models).

When this method is applied to growth, we are able to see whether the particular model of growth we have proposed simulates behaviour like the behaviour in the actual data sample. If our test does not reject the model we can have quite a lot of confidence that it is close to the truth because the test has such a high rejection rate for false models – including of course models with reverse causation (growth causing changes in taxes) or third-factor causation (growth and taxes not affecting each other but both being driven by a third variable).

The research reported in Chapters 7 and 8 (L. Minford 2015a,b) tests a model for the UK from the 1970s where tax and regulation affect growth through the incentives for entrepreneurs to innovate.

Understanding model error

In many modelling situations, when looking at the 'accuracy' of a model, we consider the 'standard error' of an estimated effect of some policy change. If we have estimated a relationship in which,

---

4 As Tolstoy put it, just as 'every unhappy family is unhappy in its own way', incorrect models of the economy are incorrect in different ways and therefore produce outcomes that vary from each other and vary from the history.

say, a 1 percentage point change in the tax rate lowers output by 0.5 per cent, then there are standard statistical formulae that tell us with some degree of statistical confidence the upper and lower bounds of that effect. However, this is not really what we want to know when we have a full model of the economy in which the policy change creates many ramifications. In this situation we want to know how 'totally wrong' we could be about the effect. The unforeseen consequences about which economists often write are not generally differences in the magnitude of the effect of a policy change on some economic variable but differences in the direction of the effect. Whether the model is likely to produce an answer that is totally wrong is related to the power of the tests used on the models: that is, how frequently the test rejects false models.

There are many ways in which models can be false and, if a model is 'false' it is difficult to know what part of it is false or the extent to which different parts are false – for example, is it the tax parameter or another parameter or both? However, this new approach to tax and growth modelling will reject false models with a high probability regardless of the source of the 'inaccuracy'.

The results of tax and growth modelling

As already noted, further results will be discussed in Chapters 7 and 8. At this stage, the most important finding is the order of magnitude of the impact of tax and regulation on growth. In this model, the combination of tax with regulation has at least two justifications. The first is that the effects can be similar – they both impose costs on businesses and, indirectly at least, employees. The second is that they can be substitutes: governments may choose to achieve a particular objective by increasing taxes or by regulating. For example, laws enforcing union powers and rises in income tax rates each redistribute resources but also in different ways reduce the return to entrepreneurial innovation and so damage growth.

The magnitude of the effect of tax and regulation on growth from this model was close to the Minford and Wang results discussed above and slightly below those that tend to be found from growth regressions.

In Part 1, it was suggested that, as far as Britain is concerned, the growth-maximising average spending ratio to is 17.5–22.5 per cent of national income and the welfare-maximising point is 27.5–32.5 per cent of national income. Broadly, the model suggests that a cut in government spending to the welfare-maximising point from current levels might imply a rise in the economic growth rate by around 1 percentage point; and a cut to the growth-maximising point would imply a rise in the economic growth rate by a further 0.8 percentage points. These are clearly orders of magnitude and the effects of cutting government spending are unlikely to be a simple linear function of the extent of the cut. However, there is a lot of evidence from different sources that points towards figures of this order.

7 TAX, REGULATION AND GROWTH: UNDERSTANDING THE RESEARCH

Lucy Minford

There is a huge empirical literature on growth and its causes. Chapter 6 examined some of the results of that literature specifically in relation to how taxes affect growth. However, one of the problems of that literature is that it is very difficult to ascertain cause and effect or which factors are the real drivers of growth. In this chapter, therefore, the economic work on the causes of growth is examined more closely. There is fuller discussion, including a review of the theoretical literature, in L. Minford (2015a).

The new work presented in Chapter 8 overcomes many of the problems in the earlier literature. It also includes the important issue of entrepreneurship and the effect of tax and regulation on growth through this channel. This chapter therefore also examines the problems in the early work on these topics.

The effect of tax on growth: further analysis of the growth regression approach

Empirical work on the macroeconomic causes of growth has been dominated by the Barro growth regression (Barro 1991), as mentioned in the preceding chapter. This involves panel analysis, using data observed for many countries (a cross-section) over time.

A cross-section is used in order to obtain counterfactual variation (what would have happened to growth had the policy experience been different?), and a larger set of countries may offer a wider variety of policy profiles, particularly for reasonably long time series. However, there is a problem in assuming that the effects of the factors are the same across a large set of countries with very different characteristics. Many of the characteristics that affect growth in different countries will be unmeasured and the effect of these factors will show up in the error term.[1] Furthermore, the sample may not be random if more of one 'type' of country with unmeasured characteristics that affect growth is included than others (Levine and Zervos 1993). There are methods used to overcome this problem. For example, more variables could be included. However, if more variables are included, there may be insufficient data to obtain robust results if the time series is short.

Another potential problem with growth regressions is that variables may be inconsistently measured across countries. This will make any cross-country policy–growth relationships even less stable or more difficult to find. Such problems have been addressed by looking at groups of 'similar' countries, for instance, an OECD sample. However, this reduces the sample size.

Even for more similar countries, many variables have been found to be correlated with growth and the temptation is to include them all in a regression. However, the variables may be highly correlated with each other. The more they are correlated with each other, the more difficult it is to distinguish the individual effects of the different variables (Loayza and Soto 2002; Brock and Durlauf 2001). On the other hand, if fewer variables are included, how do we choose which variables can reasonably be excluded?

---

1 If relevant country characteristics are fixed over time this is easy to deal with – it is when they change over time that it becomes problematic.

It has also often been found that a variable that is significant in one regression then loses its significance when included alongside additional or different regressors (Levine and Renelt 1992). This problem is often addressed by using an approach called 'extreme bounds analysis' (Leamer 1983), which checks whether the significance and magnitude of the coefficient of interest is robust when further variables are added. When such analysis is conducted, it is often found that the relationship between growth and most variables is fragile.[2]

A separate problem is so-called 'reverse causality'. What happens if the relevant variable is dependent on growth rather than growth dependent on the variable? Simple regressions might not be able to find a causal relationship from simple associations. For example, better rule of law might lead to more growth. However, more growth might lead to better capacity to run an effective and efficient legal system. Which causes which? Does the rule of law improve growth or does growth improve the rule of law? Or does the association run both ways? Similar mechanisms can be envisaged with tax and growth. For example, higher growth may give the government more space to reduce the tax burden as a proportion of national income and a reduced tax burden might increase growth. This ambiguity over the direction of causation fundamentally undermines the policy conclusions of a growth regression. If the goal is to investigate the scope for growth policy levers, Barro-type regressions may well not get us there.

When regressors are endogenous (that is, when a variable, such as tax, both affects and is affected by growth or is affected by some other variable that also affects growth) an approach known as an 'instrumental variable strategy' should be used. Many recent growth regressions take this approach. This is a complex but a widely used technique in econometrics. A variable must be found

---

2   Some argue that this is not an appropriate test, e.g. Sala-i-Martin (1994). See also Sala-i-Martin et al. (2004) for a different approach to selecting independent variables in growth regressions.

(an instrument) that is strongly correlated with the policy variable under investigation (for example, the tax rate) but which is otherwise unrelated to growth. If this variable is found to affect growth, then that effect, it is argued, must come through the influence of tax on growth – the argument has to be made theoretically.

This technique is best explained by example; the following is from Leigh and Schembri (2004), who investigate the relationship between smoking and health. In this context it might be very difficult to work out whether it really is smoking or some other variable that is affecting health (because smokers might be unhealthy in other respects or, if a time series is being used, there will be other things happening as the level of smoking changes that will also affect health). However, we could, instead, investigate the relationship between tobacco taxes and health. It seems implausible that tobacco taxes could affect health other than through their impact on smoking and so, if we find a relationship, the underlying driver of the relationship is probably changes in smoking.

It goes without saying that it is extremely difficult to apply this technique in the case of growth regressions.

More recent studies address the problem of the difficulty of disentangling cause from effect by using an approach called a 'dynamic generalised method of moments' (GMM) or GMM system approach (Arellano and Bond 1991; Blundell and Bond 1998). Even this complex approach has not proven satisfactory. Angrist and Krueger (2001) dub such identification strategies 'mechanical and naïve', relying as they do on 'atheoretical and hard-to-assess assumptions about dynamic relationships' (p. 76). Murray refers to a 'dark cloud of invalidity' hanging over the instrumental variable approach that 'never entirely goes away' (Murray 2006: 114).

When it comes to the traditional growth regression approach discussed earlier, it may not be entirely fair to conclude that 'ultimately this line of research is a dead end, if the aim is to understand what causes growth so that we can improve the situation'

(Myles 2009b: 16). But we can certainly agree with Easterly that, where growth policy is concerned, 'Regressions can be dangerous!' (Easterly 2008). They may provide useful information. But they must be treated with care. It is for this reason that the approach taken in Chapter 8 really does add something new to the debate on tax and growth.

The effect of tax on growth: further considerations

For the reasons discussed above, it is difficult to disentangle the historical relationships between tax and growth. Growth regressions certainly provide evidence of an association between various economic and political economy variables and growth but little can be concluded from them with regard to causality. There are, though, some other issues that specifically relate to the modelling of tax on growth that deserve further comment.

Marginal or average tax rates?

Many cross-country growth regressions include the overall share of tax revenue in GDP as an explanatory variable (i.e. as a variable that explains growth).[3] This measures the national average tax rate, but theory suggests that it is *marginal* tax rates that distort individual incentives so as to reduce investment and other important variables that affect growth. The impact of total tax revenue on growth is ambiguous. For example, tax revenues may be used to finance public goods which are productive inputs and help growth. This may indirectly imply a positive relationship between average tax rates and growth – at least when tax rates are low. As tax rates become higher, we would expect the total tax take to affect growth negatively and, eventually, taxes will affect growth to such an extent that the tax take is lowered

---

3   Much of this discussion follows Myles (2009a).

and government spending has to be reduced (the so-called Laffer curve effect). However, overall, theory cannot unambiguously identify whether there would be a negative or positive relationship between average tax rates and growth – it will depend on the level tax rates have reached.

Negative growth effects arise in theory not from the average tax rate but from the marginal tax rate (the proportion of income earned through an additional unit of some activity or investment that will be confiscated). Generally, for OECD economies the average and marginal tax rates are not the same, due to progressivity in the tax schedule: for a progressive tax system, the marginal tax rate is above the average rate at every income level. Since the marginal rate changes at the threshold between different income brackets, calculating the appropriate national level of the marginal rate for personal income taxes is difficult and this is made more so by exemptions or special rates for different types of income. For corporation tax, the picture is further complicated by accelerated depreciation allowances for different types of capital spending and other tax breaks, such as research and development tax credits. Some studies (Koester and Kormendi 1989; Easterly and Rebelo 1993) attempt to calculate an 'effective' marginal tax rate at the economy level, but whether these capture cross-country differences in tax design consistently is controversial.

Due to the inherent difficulties in measuring marginal tax rates the average tax rate is still widely used in studies on tax and growth. However, below, some studies are discussed which examine the impact of marginal tax rates on entrepreneurship.

Tax and growth: a two-way relationship

Many earlier studies in the tax-growth literature do not account for endogeneity bias in their estimates (Engen and Skinner 1996) – in other words, do changes in the tax burden cause growth or does growth cause a change in the tax burden? This is, of course, just a specific example of the cause-and-effect issue discussed above. The relationship between tax and growth can also be affected by the political system. Tax is a highly politicised area and rates certainly respond to political pressures, which in turn can be caused by the state of the economy.

Slemrod (1995) notes that government expenditure responds to country-level political preferences, and that the income elasticity of demand for government spending is above one (Wagner's law) – i.e. demand for goods and services funded by the government increases with development. This implies that higher growth will lead to higher levels of taxes (note, not lower levels of taxes – the positive sign of the effect contrasts with the negative relationship feeding from tax to growth which is sometimes supposed). Regressions of tax and growth that do not take this into account lead to estimates that are very difficult to interpret.

Entrepreneurship and growth

Given the problems discussed above with the tax and growth literature, one approach is to try to specify a more robust theoretical model – that is, to try to better understand the channels through which tax can affect growth. One of the main channels through which tax levels affect growth is through their impact on entrepreneurship. Thus, in tying together the issues of growth and tax, we also need to consider the relationship between entrepreneurship and growth and then examine more closely the impact of tax – together with other factors such as regulation – on entrepreneurship. Unfortunately, the work on the relationship between entrepreneurship and growth suffers from similar failings to that on the relationship between tax and growth with the additional problem that entrepreneurship is difficult to define.

Carree et al. (2002) look at the relationship between per capita GDP and business ownership in 23 OECD countries for the period 1976 to 1996. Business ownership is defined as the number of business owners in all sectors (except agriculture) as a proportion of the labour force, and therefore measures the stock of self-employed businesses rather than new business creation. The authors argue that the business ownership rate is a reasonable, though imperfect, proxy for entrepreneurship.[4] They argue that it is not so much the level of entrepreneurship (defined in this way) that leads to growth but that a deviation from the equilibrium level of self-employment that is problematic – in either direction. Having a large number of business owners is not necessarily good or bad; the problem arises when we have an economic system that leads to a higher or lower number of business owners than would exist in a world free of undesirable interventions (for example, if self-employment and small business ownership is encouraged by employment regulations on medium-sized and large businesses).

The authors put great emphasis on potential policy implications of the results, drawing on the comment from Kirzner that 'government regulation of market activity is likely to obstruct and frustrate the spontaneous, corrective forces of entrepreneurial adjustments' (Kirzner 1997: 81). In other words, free entry, and exit from the market free of stigma and financial burdens, are essential for entrepreneurship rates to be allowed to find their equilibrium in the face of shocks, and hence for economic growth to reach its potential.

Audretsch and Thurik (2001) look at the same set of 23 OECD countries within the same setup for 1974–98. They also find that any deviation from the equilibrium rate of entrepreneurship reduces growth; this holds when entrepreneurship is measured both by the self-employment rate and by the share of small firms in economic activity.

---

4   Across countries the definition of business owners differs in breadth (regarding businesses that are not legally incorporated, for instance), so they adjust the OECD statistics to correct for this. However, they note that issues remain for comparing these rates across countries.

There are a number of other studies conducted using different methods, for example that by Erken et al. (2008). The conclusion appears to be that, when a number of variables are included (for example, human capital and various R&D measures, as well as catch-up growth variables and labour participation rates), entrepreneurship is an additional factor in the productivity process alongside human capital accumulation and R&D. Acs et al. (2012) use a Barro-style regression approach as described above for 18 OECD countries. They use a range of techniques to deal with the difficulty of distinguishing between cause and effect and, even after controlling for R&D, find that entrepreneurship has a positive and significant effect on growth. The estimates for the impact of entrepreneurship are robust in different samples across different date ranges (1981–98 and 1990–98).

Both entrepreneurship and export orientation are investigated by Hessels and van Stel (2011) in a group of 34 countries from 2002 to 2008. They find that export orientation has a positive and significant additional impact on growth above the impact found for entrepreneurship, though this result is only found for high-income countries. Entrepreneurship appears as a significant cause of growth across all specifications and for all levels of income, with the magnitude slightly larger for less developed countries in the sample. The authors acknowledge that there is a small sample size used in the study.

As with the tax and growth literature, interpreting the work in this field is problematic. However, there would appear to be some indication (as we would expect) that entrepreneurship is important for growth, though we should be very careful how we measure entrepreneurship.

Linking tax to entrepreneurship in theory

There is evidence to substantiate the view that taxation reduces entrepreneurship through incentive effects – though some studies do reject this link. The impact of marginal tax rates on the aggregate level of entrepreneurship is actually ambiguous, depending on the risk attitudes of potential entrepreneurs (Gentry and Hubbard 2000). Risk-averse individuals may be more inclined to undertake uncertain entrepreneurial ventures when tax schedules are more progressive, since a more redistributive tax regime acts as insurance against failure. This would imply a positive relationship between marginal tax rates (or tax progressivity) and entrepreneurship (Domar and Musgrave 1944). While this is counter-intuitive to many people, essentially what is happening here is that, though success is taxed, failure is subsidised. However, for a risk-neutral entrepreneur higher marginal rates will reduce entry (Gentry and Hubbard 2000). Of course, the precise effect will depend on the exact shape of the tax system – the extent to which successes are taxed and the extent to which failures are cushioned.

Another channel through which tax rates on businesses (or the interaction between business taxes and other taxes) might lead to higher entrepreneurship as measured by self-employment rates is that of tax avoidance. If tax rates on business profits are lower than on wage income, individuals will move into self-employment. Though some studies use self-employment as a proxy for entrepreneurship, self-employment simply motivated by tax avoidance is often a substitute for employment rather than being an example of genuine entrepreneurship and so it is worth stressing once again that we have to be careful how we define entrepreneurship.

There is also work that looks at how specific tax policies or 'tax instruments' affect entrepreneurship levels through their effects on risk-taking (for references, see Baliamoune-Lutz and Garello 2014: 171). For example, tax instruments are often used to affect access to finance for start-ups (Gompers and Lerner 1999; Bruce and Mohsin 2006). The consensus from the evidence is that higher tax rates lead to lower venture capital funding. Asoni and

Sanandaji (2009) also propose a theoretical model in which progressive taxes reduce the average quality of firms even though entrepreneurial entry rates increase.

Marginal tax rates and entrepreneurship

As has been noted, it cannot be taken for granted that low taxes necessarily lead to more entrepreneurship. What does the empirical evidence say? Baliamoune-Lutz and Garello (2014) provide a table summarising the samples, tax regressors and qualitative results of recent empirical work on entrepreneurship and taxes for OECD countries (2014: Table 1, p. 169). They find that the sign and magnitude of the estimated effects differs both across countries and within countries or groups of countries in different studies. Two time series studies for the UK illustrate this: Parker (1996) finds a positive impact of marginal tax rates on growth, while Robson (1998) finds no effect.

Baliamoune-Lutz and Garello find that tax progressivity for above the average income brackets reduces estimated measures of nascent entrepreneurship in a study of 15 OECD countries between 2000 and 2008.[5] They note that there is a potential for two-way causality between entrepreneurship and the tax variables, since tax reforms may be a policy response to poor observed entrepreneurship outcomes.[6]

The authors of this study derive two progressivity variables. The first is the difference between the marginal tax rate applying at 100 per cent of average earnings and the marginal rate applying at 67 per cent of average earnings. The second is the difference

---

5 Nascent entrepreneurship as measured by the Global Entrepreneurship Monitor is the percentage of 18–64 population actively involved in setting up a business they own or co-own.

6 They use difference generalised method of moments, a statistical technique, to try to control for this.

between the marginal tax rates at 167 per cent and 100 per cent of average earnings. The authors find that the second of these variables is significantly negatively related to entrepreneurship, across all specifications.[7] In other words, as the tax system becomes more progressive above average earnings, entrepreneurship is reduced.

Their findings are therefore consistent with Gentry and Hubbard's micro-analysis on US data (2000, 2004). Those authors show that tax progressivity decreases nascent entrepreneurship for those who start with higher incomes. The policy implication is that reducing tax progressivity for the income bracket between 100 and 167 per cent of average earnings stimulates nascent entrepreneurship.

They note that the impact of this reform depends in practice on reforms to other factors in the entrepreneurship decision, such as regulatory costs. The entrepreneur responds to the tax schedule 'in its entirety' (their emphasis) and this includes regulatory costs which have the same effect as taxes. Deriving the effective tax rate including regulatory costs is extremely challenging. In their concluding remarks they speculate: 'it is not clear that governments should take the opposite direction and engage in positive discrimination in favour of start-ups or new businesses. It is possible that the best strategy would involve more fiscal neutrality. Low progressivity, or even a flat tax, might be part of such a strategy but it is also important to reduce the global fiscal burden and start-up costs' (p. 185).

Overall, then, this work suggests that high marginal tax rates at higher incomes reduce entrepreneurship. However, tax rates cannot be seen in isolation from other costs on business formation such as regulatory costs.

---

7   This result is robust to the use of average rather than marginal rates in calculating the progressivity indicator; the first progressivity indicator is not significant in all specifications.

Corporate taxes and entrepreneurship

We might also expect taxes on corporations to be linked to entrepreneurial incentives. Djankov et al. (2010) derive comparable effective corporate tax rates for 85 countries of different income levels in 2004. They look at how investment and entrepreneurship vary with these tax rates across countries. Entrepreneurship is measured by cross-country indicators of business density and formal entry, developed from the World Bank's Entrepreneurship Survey, which gathers data on business registration.[8] They recognise that these measures exclude informal entrepreneurship, while including businesses that go through the administrative incorporation process at a time different from when they started up. Across a variety of specifications they find a significant, negative effect of effective corporate tax rates for the top income band on both business density and entry rates, as well as on fixed capital formation in manufacturing (though not in services) and foreign direct investment: 'in these new data, corporate taxes matter a lot, and in ways consistent with basic economic theory' (p. 59).

Da Rin et al. (2011) look at the impact of lagged average effective corporate tax rates for 17 EU countries, from 1997 to 2004, on formal incorporation rates at the country–industry level. The authors acknowledge that incorporation rates could affect taxes, just as taxes could affect incorporation rates, and they use techniques to try to overcome this problem. They conclude that higher corporate tax rates reduce entry rates, though only when

---

8   Business density is the total number of registered limited liability corporations per 100 members of the working population in 2004. The rate of new business registration is new registrations as a proportion of total registrations averaged between 2000 and 2004. The data exclude sole proprietorships, i.e. 15.1 million businesses in the US as of 2010; however, their tax regime is different so their inclusion would inappropriate.

tax rates are below a threshold level. This holds across a range of models.

Overall, the work on corporate taxes seems unambiguous. In most situations, higher corporate taxes are associated with lower business formation. While it is worth reiterating that these studies are subject to limitations discussed earlier in the chapter – specifically that they do not demonstrate causation from tax to business formation – it would be reasonable to hypothesise that this is a channel through which taxes *could* reduce entrepreneurship and economic growth. The work in Chapter 8 investigates that hypothesis.

Concluding remarks on taxation and entrepreneurship

Overall, in the earlier literature, there is no robust empirical evidence that economic growth is causally related to the level of aggregate taxation. Although that avenue of research seemed promising, it runs into the many problems that have been discussed above. Of course, that does not mean that the aggregate tax burden is not causally related to growth, but the estimation techniques that have been used are not sufficiently robust to uncover such a relationship with certainty.

It would seem plausible that growth is responsive to the level of taxation – especially starting at current levels – for reasons discussed in Chapter 1. We would particularly expect growth to be sensitive to high marginal tax rates. For example, corporation tax may well affect growth through the channels of investment and entrepreneurship. The same may well apply to the higher marginal rates of income tax. However, there are alternative theories that might suggest that higher taxes can promote growth via various channels, at least up to a point.

Further work is needed to obtain more persuasive evidence that a reduction in taxes can lead to higher growth. The results presented in Chapter 8 provides such evidence.

Labour market regulation and growth

The importance of labour market regulation

Labour market regulation can be thought of as the laws and institutions intended to protect the interests of workers.[9] In addition to certain civil rights protections, it includes employment law, collective relations law and social security provisions. Every OECD country intervenes in labour markets. Such interventions can improve welfare and also improve growth where they resolve genuine market failures. However, they may also introduce frictions. The focus of this section is on those frictions and their potential growth effects.

The practical impact of labour market regulation on market outcomes depends not just on the laws and regulations themselves but on how legislation, contracts and agreements are interpreted and enforced by the authorities responsible, as well as on how compliance is monitored. This enforcement factor is not static over time. Unfortunately, no measures exist of regulatory enforcement quality over time for OECD countries (certainly not for the UK over the period from 1970 to 2009) so this dimension of the problem cannot easily be examined empirically.

The theoretical direction of the growth effect of labour market regulation is ambiguous. It may be that some employment protection legislation (EPL) increases investment in skills due to increased job tenure, leading to higher productivity growth via human capital accumulation (Damiani and Pompei 2010; Belot et al. 2007). On the other hand, higher regulation raises the costs of labour adjustment leading to labour market inefficiency (e.g. Mortensen and Pissarides 1994; Hopenhayn and Rogerson 1993), and may pose a barrier to the adoption of new technology requiring new skillsets. Labour market regulation may also reduce

---

9 Botero et al. (2004: 1339). Of course, whether they do actually protect the interests of workers is a different point.

productivity by affecting a firm's choice of projects – by increasing anticipated costs of labour adjustment, high hiring and firing costs may lead to the selection of lower-risk, lower-productivity projects as opposed to more radical innovations with higher associated risk (Saint-Paul 2002; Bartelsman et al. 2004).[10] Another productivity dampening effect of employment protection legislation is the potential for workers to increase absenteeism or reduce work effort due to the lower threat of dismissal.[11]

Labour market regulation is relevant to a broad discussion of tax and growth. In many cases, labour market regulation may have the same effects as a tax – it increases the cost of employment. Also, labour market regulation can act as a substitute for tax. For example, the government might try to achieve by regulation goals that it might otherwise have sought to achieve by taxation and the provision of subsidies. Indeed, the proponents of recent increases in the minimum wage in the UK have directly employed that argument.

Empirical evidence on labour market regulation

As with many of the other determinants of growth that have been discussed, when it comes to labour market regulation, there is the potential for reverse causality. In other words, though it is true that labour market regulation might affect growth, the level of national income may well help determine the extent of labour market regulation.[12] This might happen through various channels. Notwithstanding this, various studies suggest that labour market

---

10 For cross-country evidence that EPL hampers the adjustment process of productivity and employment after shocks, see Burgess et al. (2000) and Caballero et al. (2004).

11 For more discussion of the theoretical literature on how regulation may affect labour market outcomes and hence productivity, see Bassanini et al. (2009: 358–61).

12 Indeed, the influential paper by Botero et al. (2004) investigates how income determines EPL rather than the reverse.

regulation is negatively associated with workforce participation and youth unemployment. Cause and effect are not, however, distinguished effectively in much of the work on these issues.

In general, the empirical literature does not offer a firm consensus one way or another on the direction of impact of LMR on economic growth or on employment (Frontier Economics 2012). Whether it affects particular types of employment (for example, youth employment or long-term unemployment) is a different matter and not one considered here. DeFreitas and Marshall (1998) conduct an industry-level study (limited to manufacturing) for a sample of Latin American and Asian countries, and find that increasing the stringency of employment protection legislation reduces labour productivity growth. However, studies of OECD countries by Nickell and Layard (1999) and Koeniger (2005) point to a weak but positive effect of raising the stringency of EPL on both total factor productivity (TFP) growth and R&D intensity. Though, of course, overall growth is determined by productivity and the level of employment (among other things) and it might be the case that labour market regulation increases productivity by excluding the least productive members of the labour force.

Di Tella and MacCulloch (2005) examine the impact of survey-based indices of hiring and firing regulations on labour market outcomes for 21 OECD countries between 1984 and 1990. The regulatory indicators are based on the Global Competitiveness Report (published by the World Economic Forum), which surveys groups of business managers on the labour market conditions they face. They find that higher labour market flexibility is positively associated with the employment rate and with labour force participation. Their estimates suggest that the difference in employment rates between France and the US would decrease by 14 per cent if France were to reduce regulatory strictness in the labour market to the US level. These results are in line with the earlier conclusions of Lazear (1990), who found in a panel of 22 developed countries that severance pay and required notice periods were positively related to unemployment rates. The implication of that study is that the strictness of such regulations (or perceptions of it) do affect the hiring and firing decisions of firms.

Bassanini et al. (2009) use country-level data on EPL and industry-level productivity data for 11 OECD countries and 19 industries, 1982–2003, arguing that the impact of EPL is likely to vary for different industries within the same country.[13] They argue that the impact of reforms on productivity will be greater in industries where, in the absence of regulations, firms rely on layoffs to make staffing changes, rather than in industries where internal labour markets or voluntary turnover are more important. Their estimates suggest that mandatory dismissal regulations in OECD countries reduce TFP growth in industries with a high 'natural' rate of dismissal (as proxied by the US rate), to a disproportionate degree. This result is robust to sensitivity analysis surrounding the indicators and control variables.

However, they also note the importance of various political economy arguments that suggest that changes in TFP might affect the extent of regulation. For example, there may be political pressure to protect jobs during a downturn, so that poorer economic performance leads to more employment protection legislation. Alternatively, some suggest that liberalising reforms are more frequently and easily implemented during economic crises (Drazen and Easterly 2001). Equally, reforms may be more likely to be implemented when the labour market is buoyant because the impact of reforms would be reduced. Through both channels, there might be a causal relationship between economic growth and labour market regulation. These features of the political process will make it difficult to distinguish cause from effect.

---

13 The data used for industry-level TFP are taken from Inklaar and Timmer (2008), and indicators of EPL are the OECD indicators (OECD 2004): index of dismissal for regular employment, index for temporary contracts, and index on additional legislation for concerning collective dismissals.

Bassanini et al. (2009) do use various techniques to try to overcome these problems and, overall, their evidence would seem to be robust.[14] Their estimates imply that a 1 percentage point reduction in the stringency of employment protection legislation related to regular employment contracts will raise aggregate labour productivity growth by 0.14 percentage points.

While Bassanini et al. (2009) look at the productivity effects of employment protection legislation, they do not distinguish between new and incumbent or small and larger firms. Millan et al. (2013) look at the impact of EPL on the smallest firms in a microeconometric study of individual-level data for the EU-15 countries over the period 1994–2001. They find that EPL stringency negatively affects the hiring and firing decisions of firms with one to four employees (i.e. the probabilities of employing new workers and dismissing current workers are both reduced), thus reducing labour flexibility for this class of firm. They emphasise the scale disadvantage applying to small firms in complying with EPL, since hiring and firing costs constitute a bigger proportion of overall labour costs, and there is less potential to redirect underperforming workers into different roles within the firm.

Van Stel and Thurik (2007) look at the impact of regulation on nascent entrepreneurship (the proportion of the adult population actively involved in starting a new venture) and on the conversion of nascent entrepreneurship into young entrepreneurship (the proportion of owner/managers of a business that is under 42 months old) using data from 39 countries for 2002–5. The regulatory indicators are from the World Bank Doing Business Indicators. They find that employment protection legislation has a negative and significant impact on entrepreneurship rates.

---

14 The authors note that the robustness of these results depends on whether they have chosen good instruments; again we are at the mercy of Murray's 'dark cloud' of instrument invalidity.

Conclusion

There is a great deal of work on the impact of tax and regulation on economic growth and entrepreneurship. This work should be regarded as indicative rather than definitive. There are a number of problems inherent in this research, one of the most important being that it fails to distinguish between cause and effect.

Better statistical techniques have been used, but they have their own problems. It is for this reason that further modelling has been undertaken (see Chapter 8). This modelling requires a more rounded understanding of the channels by which tax and other variables affect growth. It seems clear that an important channel is that of entrepreneurship. Entrepreneurship is difficult to measure and model, but the work that has been done suggests that high marginal tax rates at high incomes affect entrepreneurship. Furthermore, regulation that promotes either more or less self-employment or firm formation than would take place in a market without intervention tends to affect growth. Regulation of the labour market – which is often a substitute for taxes – also seems to affect growth.

The key is to tie these processes together in an analysis which unambiguously models the impact of entrepreneurship and the factors that affect it on growth, within a full account of the macroeconomy.

8 TAX, REGULATION, INCENTIVES AND GROWTH: NEW MODELLING FOR THE UK

Lucy Minford

Entrepreneurship involves implementing new ideas in markets. If policy creates large frictions in this process, then a proportion of innovative ideas will fail to be translated into productivity growth. Further, the contention in this chapter is that for entrepreneurship to drive productivity growth, markets must be competitive. An uncompetitive market offers little reward for entrants to implement new ideas or to exploit perceived opportunities, so entrepreneurship and competition go hand-in-hand. If regulation acts as a barrier to entry, it will reduce both competition and entrepreneurship. If the entrepreneur cannot keep the rewards from implementing ideas because they are taken in tax or compliance costs, this will also discourage entrepreneurship.

In some new economic growth literature, entrepreneurs play a prominent role, particularly in the knowledge spillover theory of entrepreneurship. This characterises the entrepreneur as the conduit through which spillovers from established firms' research and development raise economy-wide productivity (Acs et al. 2009). This theory recommends the removal of policy-induced 'barriers to entrepreneurship', including regulatory obstacles, excessive bureaucracy, taxes and labour market rigidities, all of which increase operational costs and uncertainty for the entrepreneur.

Although we can point this out, determining the magnitude of the effects of changing tax rates and regulation on entrepreneurship and growth is not straightforward for the reasons discussed in the previous chapter. In this chapter a model is presented that will better isolate the effect of barriers to entrepreneurship on growth. This model is subjected to a powerful test. The technique used tends to reject false models very firmly. Therefore, if its assumptions about the role of barriers to entrepreneurship in growth are not right, the model will be rejected. The model is also effective at distinguishing cause from effect.

A model with productivity driven by policy

The model used here is known as an 'open economy real business cycle model' – see Meenagh et al. (2010) – with the addition of an endogenous growth process along the lines of Meenagh et al. (2007). This is explained more fully in L. Minford (2015a,b). What are these models in plain English and how do we test them?

Recent work in macroeconomics has followed the approach known as dynamic stochastic general equilibrium (DSGE) modelling and tended to use the approach to testing originally due to Milton Friedman (1953). In this approach the model used is kept as simple as possible, so that its workings can be easily understood. It is then confronted with the data to see if the model can explain the data. It is not the realism of the model that is necessarily important but whether it explains the data.

This approach can follow two main paths. One is to ask whether the model could closely 'forecast the past': this is a familiar method which relies on the size of the forecasting errors over the past and hence their likelihood. We do not use it here because such tests tend not to be as difficult to pass when the model has first been estimated on a small sample of data.

Another more recent method allows a tougher and more discriminating test to be used. This involves seeing how the data behave according to some descriptive equations which relates the variables under consideration to their past values. This is known as a vector autoregressive (VAR) model; it is used simply to summarise the data's behaviour and is not based on any theory.

Assumptions about household behaviour

In this model it is assumed that there is a typical household and also a typical firm. The household determines its optimal consumption and labour supply behaviour to maximise utility; the firm determines how much labour to hire from the household and its investment plans in order to maximise profits. Investment is financed by the firm borrowing from the household. Whatever profits the firm makes are transferred back to their owners as dividends. Of course, those owners are also households. The economy consists of a lot of these typical household–firm pairs. To obtain the aggregate behaviour of the economy we simply multiply the behaviour of a typical pair by the numbers of them in the economy. The economy is assumed to be open to trade and also to foreign capital flows (in both directions). The growth process consists of the typical household (that owns its firm) spending time in an entrepreneurial role innovating, instead of as a worker hired for production. When it spends this time innovating it generates productivity growth for its firm.[1] It chooses how much time to spend on innovation according to the trade-off between the higher expected return from this productivity growth coming via higher dividends and the sacrifice of ordinary labour income.

From these maximising decisions come a series of equations for consumer and producer behaviour which can be summarised as follows:

• Consumption increases if real interest rates fall and if future income rises.

---

1 Note, productivity is not treated as a public good in this model and so there is no spillover.

- Investment increases if real interest rates fall and if expected future productivity increases.
- Innovation falls if tax and regulation rise because they lower its expected net return.
- Domestic real interest rates are driven to be equal to foreign real interest rates plus expected real exchange rate depreciation.
- Consumption of domestic relative to foreign products by home and foreign households rises if there is a fall in the relative price of domestic products, i.e. a fall in the real exchange rate.

These equations form the model. In addition, the model assumes that expectations are formed 'rationally', which means that they are consistent with the model's forecasts.[2] There are shocks to the model every period, generated by what are known as 'error processes'. These are the gap between what each model equation says and what the actual data implies. We can think of these gaps as the implied aspects omitted from the model that drive the economy.

How is the model tested?

When it comes to the variables that drive the model, they are assumed to follow what are known as 'auto-regressive' processes that we observe from their past behaviour. By this we mean that the behaviour of each variable depends on its own past behaviour. When one of these variables, changes (for example, if there is an unexpected rise in consumption) we tend to observe that the effect of this shock continues into the following periods but to a reduced extent.

---

2   To emphasise, it is not the intention to have a model which is 'realistic' at a detailed level, but one which is a good approximation to the average behaviour in the economy – 'good' in the sense that such a model can generate behaviour that is close to that which is actually observed.

The resulting model consists of a complete account of the economy. Different models will include different equations and variables, with the forecast errors implicitly representing the behaviour of those economic factors outside the model. Different models therefore, when simulated, generate quite different versions of what might happen in an economy (conditional on that model being correct). The implications of each distinct model can then be compared with the actual data in a formal test – at its best, this process allows us to choose between models according to their test performance.

In the 'indirect inference' test procedure, we compare the behaviour of the model with the actual data and, if the probability of observing the actual data is low according to the model, we reject the model. This indirect inference test is an extremely powerful test which tends to be effective in rejecting false models.

This model has been chosen as an appropriate backdrop against which to examine the relationship in the UK data between certain government policies and macroeconomic aggregates. The growth process is similar to Lucas (1990), in that productivity growth depends on investments of time in innovative activity. While growth in Lucas (1990) is driven by human capital accumulation, here the growth mechanism is less specifically defined and is characterised ultimately by incentives. Temporary shocks relating to the policy variable are assumed to have highly persistent effects so that there can be medium-run increases above or decreases below trend growth, even though the long-run rate of productivity growth is unchanged. This means that policy has transitional and reasonably long-lasting effects on growth, as well as permanent effects on the level of output through these shocks to growth.

We examine whether the model we have just described can accommodate the behaviour of productivity and output in the UK between 1970 and 2009. Though a shorter sample would offer a richer set of potential indicators of the policy environment faced by entrepreneurs, a longer time series dataset captures greater variation in policy behaviour within the UK. The 1970s reflect a policy regime in the UK in sharp contrast to the supply-side reforms of the 1980s and 1990s, and its inclusion adds significantly to the variation in the sample data which can be used to estimate and test the model.

The policy variables driving productivity

According to the model, government policy is a systematic driver of the level of productivity via the entrepreneurial activities which it either stimulates or discourages. In theory, it might be possible to construct a general variable which represents a set of policies that can disincentivise entrepreneurial activities. This variable could embrace any policy-related factor that reduces the expected return to entrepreneurial activities, or that raises the uncertainty attached to returns from entrepreneurship. We can also think of this policy variable as reflecting the extent to which the returns from higher productivity resulting from entrepreneurial activity are not appropriated by the entrepreneur responsible for generating them. There are many possible variables, but we only model tax and regulation, the main issues discussed in Chapter 7.

Entrepreneurship is loosely defined following the synthesis of the entrepreneurship literature in Wennekers and Thurik (1999: 46–47) as the 'ability and willingness [...] to perceive and create new economic opportunities [...] and to introduce their ideas in the market, in the face of uncertainty and other obstacles [...] it implies participation in the competitive process'. Clearly, this embraces diverse activities for which the policy-related incentives are numerous and interact in complex ways (for example, it might include the complexity of the tax system for micro-businesses which itself might depend on the general level of regulation in the economy and the level of taxes). Rich time series data on business environments, such as the World Bank's Doing Business indicators, have only been systematically collected in recent years. Where pre-1990s' data exist on the regulatory burdens surrounding business activities, they are patchy.

There is a distinction between productive and unproductive entrepreneurship (Baumol 1990). Excessive regulatory or tax burdens can lead to unproductive entrepreneurship as individuals divert energy to avoidance or evasion, or to lobbying for the removal of regulation and tax burdens. Hence, the removal of such burdens should stimulate productivity growth. On the other hand, the introduction of subsidy programmes explicitly designed to incentivise entrepreneurship may lead to business start-ups that are not innovative and make no contribution to productivity growth, though they may reduce unemployment. For this reason, measures of new business creation or self-employment rates could be poor proxies for entrepreneurship as they group together both innovative and non-innovative start-ups or small businesses together, while only a subset of these generate productivity growth. Thus, the chosen policy variables should capture only those aspects of the policy environment that lead to innovative business activity.

For example, we would want to exclude from the policy variable the incentive, noted by Crawford and Freedman (2010), for an employee to become self-employed or for a self-employed person to incorporate purely for tax arbitrage purposes – since the activity undertaken is unchanged, there is no impact on productivity from changes in the incentives around its formal categorisation.

In practice, some policy measures which enhance productive entrepreneurship in some individuals may simultaneously encourage unproductive entrepreneurship in others. At the aggregate level the focus is on the net impact of such policies on growth. If the net effect of cuts in the regulatory and tax burdens identified is to persuade people into entrepreneurial activities which are less innovative or more risky, then we will find a negative relationship between the policy variable and entrepreneurship, and this model, which suggests a positive relationship, will be rejected by the data.

Data for the policy variable

The underlying assumption in the model is that incentives affect growth through entrepreneurship. Those incentives are determined broadly by the tax and regulatory environment, which is multifaceted. However, if we try to incorporate too many of these aspects of the policy environment in one index, we risk obscuring the policy conclusions, since various aspects could offset one another within the index. For these reasons, the model uses a single policy index variable, made up of just a few key components suspected to affect entrepreneurship.

Measuring regulation

The UK index for the policy variable falls into two parts: regulation and tax. On regulation, the focus (due to data range and availability) is on the labour market. Two components from the labour market subsection of the Economic Freedom of the World (EFW) indicators compiled by the Fraser Institute were used: the Centralized Collective Bargaining (CCB) index and the Mandated Cost of Hiring (MCH) index.[3] Of the labour market measures, these two components span the longest time frame: each is measured from 1970. The original data source for the CCB index is the World Economic Forum's Global Competitiveness Report (various issues), where survey participants answer the following question: 'Wages in your country are set by a centralized

---

3   The EFW indicators are widely used in peer-reviewed empirical research; we have also conducted sensitivity tests around the indicators described in this section, and the conclusions are robust.

bargaining process (= 1) or up to each individual company (= 7).[4] The Fraser Institute converts these scores onto a [0,10] interval.

The MCH index is based on data from the World Bank's Doing Business project, and reflects 'the cost of all social security and payroll taxes and the cost of other mandated benefits including those for retirement, sickness, healthcare, maternity leave, family allowance, and paid vacations and holidays associated with hiring an employee' (Fraser Institute 2009). These costs are also converted to a [0,10] interval. These [0,10] scores are scaled to a [0,1] interval in our study.[5]

The information from the CCB and MCH indicators is used to create an index of labour market inefficiency, which is high when labour markets are inflexible: we label this the 'Labour Market Regulation' indicator (LMR).[6] (See Figure 17.)

Other types of regulation are not incorporated into the policy indicator. Not only are good quality measures largely unavailable spanning the full period under analysis but, as stated earlier, the inclusion of too many distinct series within the variable makes the policy interpretations of the test less clear. However, it is interesting to note that the correlation between the Fraser Institute measures of CCB and MCH and the OECD indicator of Product Market Regulation (PMR) is of the order of 0.8 or above. This suggests that the LMR indicator 'moves together' with product market entry regulation during the sample period. However, we

---

4   The precise wording of this question has differed slightly for different years.

5   The data from the Fraser Institute are also adjusted using information obtained from data on UK trade union membership (TUM) in order to provide more reliable data at greater frequency.

6   A full measure of regulatory burden in labour markets would also reflect all areas of employment protection legislation including costs of firing (see, for example, Botero et al. 2004), but data availability is a constraint. Correlations of our LMR indicators with OECD measures of EPL from 1985 for the UK are actually negative; our indicators do not fully capture the increases in dismissal regulation over the period and thus may slightly overstate the extent to which the UK labour market is 'deregulated'; however, the strong decline of collective bargaining and union power over the period represents the removal of significant labour market frictions.

should not overstate the power of the LMR indicator to represent the regulatory landscape as a whole. For example, environmental regulation and planning regulations are excluded, as is the impact of regulatory enforcement. Planning regulations in particular are thought to pose a serious barrier to UK businesses and one that has not been reduced significantly over the sample period (Crafts 2006; Frontier Economics 2012). Nevertheless, this regulatory indicator captures the general trend in UK policy, which has been to lower some important regulatory barriers to entrepreneurship relative to their 1970 level.

Measuring taxation

The second part of the barriers-to-entrepreneurship variable reflects the tax environment faced by the would-be entrepreneur. This environment is highly complex at the microeconomic level, depending on the inter-relationships between numerous individual tax and subsidy instruments, many of which were not in force throughout the full sample period. In the absence of a comprehensive measure of the 'effective' tax rate on the entrepreneur for the period from 1970 to 2009, the top marginal income tax rate is used as a proxy for the extent to which the proceeds of entrepreneurial endeavour are not appropriable by the individual entrepreneur. This approach is taken by others such as Lee and Gordon (2005). The top marginal rate is measured as the tax rate incurred on an additional unit of income at the threshold of the top band, however the top band is defined in each period.[7] This is not to say that every entrepreneur gets into the top income tax bracket; many entrepreneurial ventures fail or make little profit, and the expected return to entrepreneurship is generally small. However, the top marginal tax rate is intended as a proxy for the

---

7 Since the level of progressivity in the income tax schedule changes considerably over the sample period, the definition of the top band varies and that variation is not captured in this measure.

Figure 17 Labour market regulation, top marginal income tax and corporation tax rates

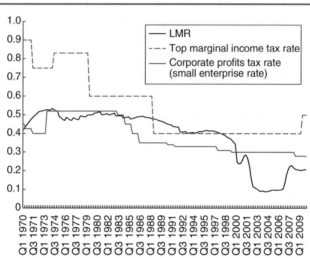

profit motive that is central to the notion of entrepreneurship, as we have defined it. Other empirical work suggests that this is appropriate.[8]

There may be an argument for including the SME rate of corporation tax in the index, on the basis that reductions in this rate lower the costs of running a new business. An argument against assuming that lower corporation tax might enhance productive entrepreneurship is that, as mentioned above, reducing corporation tax relative to other forms of taxation (employee or self-employed labour income) distorts incentives to incorporate at the small end of the business size distribution in a way that has nothing to do with productivity growth. This seems to have happened in the UK when the SME corporation tax rate and starting

---

8 Note the result in Baliamoune-Lutz and Garello (2014) that a reduction in marginal tax rates at the top of the income distribution relative to the marginal tax rate at average earnings increases entrepreneurship.

rate on profits under £10,000 were repeatedly cut between 1997 and 2002 (Crawford and Freedman 2010). Therefore the corporation tax rate has not been included in the main policy variable index. However, an alternative policy variable constructed from the labour market indicator and the corporation tax rate (in place of the top marginal income tax rate) has been used to check the robustness of the results.

The top marginal income tax rate is measured annually. Between measurement points it is constant until policy changes. The series falls consistently over the sample period until 2009 with the introduction of the 50p tax rate on income over £150,000.

The behaviour of the tax and regulatory variables

The tax and regulatory components of the policy variable indices are plotted in Figure 17. The correlations between top marginal income tax rates, the corporation tax rate and the two labour market regulation indicators are shown in Table 17.

The high positive correlation between the series support the decision to combine the labour market regulation indicator and the top marginal income tax rate in a simple average. This equally weighted combination is the main index that proxies barriers to entrepreneurship in the empirical work below. The main index is plotted in Figure 18.

The index that combines the regulatory variable with the income tax rate falls over most of the sample period. It does not fall smoothly, largely because any changes in tax rates occur at irregular intervals and can often be quite substantial. From the point of view of investigating the effect of tax and regulation on growth, the important point is that there is a lot of movement around the general trend and this helps us to produce a viable model to examine the effect of changes in the tax and regulation variable. The key issue is whether such movements actually cause changes in productivity growth.

Table 17   Correlation coefficients for tax and regulatory components of composite index

	Centralised collective bargaining	Mandated cost of hiring
Top marginal income tax rates	0.786	0.623
Corporate tax (SME rate)	0.868	0.700

Note: (1 = measures are perfectly correlated, 0 = uncorrelated and negative value means that an increase in one of the variables tends to be associated with a decrease in the other).

Tests of the model

In order to test the model, as well as the main index discussed above, results were calculated for two other measures of the tax and regulatory variable. As such, the first variable used is an equally weighted average of the labour market regulation index and the top marginal tax rate on personal income (the main index). The focus of our discussion will be on the results using this variable. The other two variables are used as tests of robustness. The second variable that is used is a combination of the labour market regulation index and the small company tax rate on corporate profits. And the third variable is the labour market regulation index alone.

The model test results suggest a high degree of confidence that the model is a good approximation of the underlying reality. The results from estimating the model led to a comfortable non-rejection[9] for the UK output and TFP behaviour. As well as being effective at explaining growth and productivity, the model performed well when assessed for its ability to match the behaviour of a variety of variables – not just productivity and output but also real interest rate and real exchange rate behaviour, as well as physical capital, labour supply and consumption in various combinations.

---

9   It is common to talk about 'non-rejection' rather than 'acceptance'. There might be other models that describe the behaviour of the economy too. The point is that, in statistical terms, the evidence suggests that this model cannot be rejected.

Figure 18 The overall barriers to entrepreneurship measure

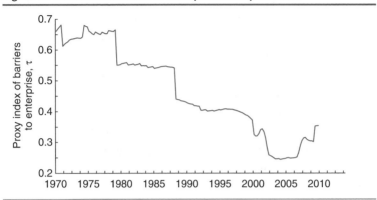

There is further discussion of these issues in L. Minford (2015a,b). Further checks on the robustness of the results show that non-rejection of the model is not sensitive to the composition of the policy index.[10] However, the inclusion of the top marginal income tax rate, with its large step changes, does get the model closer to the data.

Results: the impact of regulation and tax on growth

What interests us most about tax and regulatory policy in the UK growth model is what will happen when there is (for example) a 10 percentage point fall in the measured tax/regulation rate relative to the trend change in the variable. The model suggests that the effect of a 10 percentage point fall in the de-trended tax–regulation variable in a given quarter dies out over around ten years. In other words, the change that is modelled is not a permanent change. In line with what tends to happen in practice in a country governed by a democracy, the model examines what will happen to growth if

---

10 Further sensitivity tests were also done around the construction and interpolation of the labour market index components.

a government reduces taxes or regulation, but where the tax level goes back to its long-run trend over ten years.

Such a 10 percentage point reduction in the index of tax and regulation produces a rise in output over about thirty years of 24 per cent. This is equivalent to a higher growth rate over a thirty-year 'growth episode' following the cut of about 0.8 percentage points per annum (an 'elasticity' of 0.16). The reason that the consequence of the change is spread over such a long period is likely to be that capital accumulation and the effects of capital accumulation take a long time to react fully to the rise in total factor productivity produced by the tax change. In other words, the impact of the tax change is substantial and long lasting.

It is not possible, formally, to separate out the effects of the tax component and the regulatory component of the barriers to entrepreneurship index because the model was only fully estimated for the combined index – tax might be more important in affecting growth than regulation or it may be the other way round: it is impossible to tell. However, when we look at the barriers to entrepreneurship index itself, changes in the tax rate are driving most of the change in the index. As such, and given other tests that have been done on the model, it would not be unreasonable to conclude that the impact of the tax–regulation index that we see here is driven to a substantial degree by changes in tax rates.[11]

---

11 It is important to note that the change in the tax-regulation index is a change in addition to the change which is already occurring due to downward trend in the index. The 10 percentage point reduction in the policy index is a shock on top of the systematic (or 'deterministic') reduction which tends to happen each period in the sample. Therefore, for a policymaker to obtain the simulated impact of a 10 percentage points shock on the growth rate, they would need to reduce the tax–regulatory policy variable in absolute terms by more than 10 percentage points given that the trend is downwards. In other words, the model is testing what will happen to growth if policymakers do something over and above the natural trends that are happening in policy anyway.

What can we say about the effect of tax alone? Technically, nothing of a quantitative nature. In this model, growth is driven by barriers to entrepreneurship, and both tax and regulation form such barriers. However, given that changes in the tax–regulation index are driven to a substantial degree by changes in tax rates, it is highly likely that an unexpected change in top marginal tax rates would affect growth. For the barriers to entrepreneurship index to be so strongly related to growth and yet for the main variable driving change in the index not to be related to growth is implausible. The index is a proxy for barriers to entrepreneurship and tax is one of those barriers.

But, given the use of regulation as an alternative to or complement to tax policies, there is a strong case for modelling both together as has been done here.

Of less importance is the estimated immediate marginal impact of the tax–regulation policy variable on the change in productivity. This was found to be −0.12, implying that a 1 percentage point reduction in the tax–regulation variable increases productivity growth in the next quarter by 0.12 percentage points. This is a very considerable effect. However, it is the longer-run effect on economic growth that is more important.

Conclusion

In this chapter, a model of the economy has been developed in which productivity growth is partly driven by temporary movements in tax and regulatory policy around a long-run trend. The impact on productivity growth arises from incentive effects on innovative entrepreneurial activity. The model has been tested over the period from 1970 to 2009 (L. Minford 2015b). The tax and regulatory policy environment for this period is proxied by an equally weighted combination of the top marginal rate of personal income tax and a labour market regulation index. The latter is a combination of a survey-based centralised collective bargaining indicator and an index of the mandated cost of hiring calculated by the World Bank. This tax and regulation index, which can be regarded as a proxy for 'barriers to entrepreneurship', does have an effect on growth. This is not a controversial finding in the context of the literature – much empirical work on OECD samples has reached similar conclusions – but the methodology used here renders these results less open to the criticisms commonly levelled at existing work in this area, since it cannot be argued that reverse causality is at work.

REFERENCES

Acs, Z. J., Braunerhjelm, P., Audretsch, D. and Carlsson, B. (2009) The knowledge spillover theory of entrepreneurship. *Small Business Economics* 32(1): 15–30.

Acs, Z., Audretsch, D., Braunerhjelm, P. and Carlsson, B. (2012) Growth and entrepreneurship. *Small Business Economics* 39(2): 289–300.

Afonso, A. and Furceri, D. (2010) Government size, composition, volatility and economic growth. *European Journal of Political Economy* 26: 517–32.

Aghion, P. and Howitt, P. (1998) *Endogenous Growth Theory*. Cambridge, MA: MIT Press.

Alesina, A., Ardagna, S., Perotti, R. and Schiantarelli, F. (2002) Fiscal policy, profits, and investment. *American Economic Review* 92: 571–89.

Angrist, J. and Krueger, A. (2001) Instrumental variables and the search for identification: from supply and demand to natural experiments. *Journal of Economic Perspectives* 15(4): 69–85.

Arellano, M. and Bond, S. (1991) Some tests of specification for panel data: Monte Carlo evidence and an application to employment equations. *Review of Economic Studies* 58: 277–97.

Asoni, A. and Sanandaji, T. (2009) Taxation and the quality of entrepreneurship. Working Paper Series 813, Research Institute of Industrial Economics.

Audretsch, D. B. and Thurik, R. (2001) Linking entrepreneurship to growth. OECD Science, Technology and Industry Working Papers 2001/2.

Baliamoune-Lutz, M. and Garello, P. (2014) Tax structure and entrepreneurship. *Small Business Economics* 42(1): 165–90.

Barro, R. J. (1991) Economic growth in a cross section of countries. *Quarterly Journal of Economics* 106: 407–43.

Bartelsman, E., Bassanini, A., Haltiwanger, J., Jarmin, R., Scarpetta, S. and Schank, T. (2004) The spread of ICT and productivity growth: is Europe really lagging behind in the new economy? In *The ICT Revolution: Productivity Differences and the Digital Divide* (ed. D. Cohen, P. Garibaldi and S. Scarpetta). Oxford University Press.

Bassanini, A. and Scarpettta, S. (2001) Does human capital matter for growth in OECD countries? Evidence from PMG estimates. OECD Economics Department Working Paper 282.

Bassanini, A., Nunziata, L. and Venn, D. (2009) Job protection legislation and productivity growth in OECD countries. *Economic Policy* 24: 349–402.

Baumol, W. J. (1990) Entrepreneurship: productive, unproductive and destructive. *Journal of Political Economy* 98: 893–921.

Belot, M., Boone, J. and van Ours, J. C. (2007) Welfare effects of employment protection. *Economica* 74: 381–96.

Bleaney, M., Gemmell, N. and Kneller, R. (2000) Testing the endogenous growth model: public expenditure, taxation and growth over the long run. *Canadian Journal of Economics* 34(1): 36–57.

Blundell, R. and Bond, S. (1998) Initial conditions and moment restrictions in dynamic panel data models. *Journal of Econometrics* 87: 115–43.

Botero, J., Djankov, S., La Porta, R. and Lopez-De-Silanes, F. C. (2004) The regulation of labor. *Quarterly Journal of Economics* 119: 1339–82.

Brock, W. A. and Durlauf, S. (2001) Growth empirics and reality. *World Bank Economic Review* 15: 229–72.

Bruce, D. and Mohsin, M. (2006) Tax policy and entrepreneurship: new time series evidence. *Small Business Economics* 16: 409–25.

Burgess, S., Knetter, M. and Michelacci, C. (2000) Employment and output adjustment in the OECD: a disaggregate analysis of the role of job security provisions. *Economica* 67: 419–35.

Caballero, R., Cowan, K., Engel, E. and Micco, A. (2004) Effective labor regulation and microeconomic flexibility. Cowles Foundation Discussion Papers 1480.

Carree, M., van Stel, A., Thurik, R. and Wennekers, S. (2002) Economic development and business ownership: an analysis using data of 23 OECD countries in the period 1976–1996. *Small Business Economics* 19(3): 271–90.

Cashin, P. (1995) Government spending, taxes and economic growth. *IMF Staff Papers* 42(2): 237–69.

Crafts, N. (2006) Regulation and productivity performance. *Oxford Review of Economic Policy* 22(2): 186–202.

Crawford, C. and Freedman, J. (2010) Small business taxation. In *Dimensions of Tax Design: The Mirrlees Review* (ed. J. Mirrlees, S. Adam, T. Besley, R. Blundell, S. Bond, R. Chote, M. Gammie, P. Johnson, G. Myles and J. Poterba). Oxford University Press for Institute for Fiscal Studies.

Da Rin, M., Di Giacomo, M. and Sembe, A. (2011) Entrepreneurship, firm entry, and the taxation of corporate income: evidence from Europe. *Journal of Public Economics* 95: 1048–66.

Damiani, M. and Pompei, F. (2010) Labour protection and productivity in EU economies: 1995–2005. *European Journal of Comparative Economics* 7(2): 373–411.

DeFreitas, G. and Marshall, A. (1998) Labour surplus, worker rights and productivity growth: a comparative analysis of Asia and Latin America. *Labour* 12: 515–39.

Di Tella, R. and MacCulloch, R. (2005) The consequences of labor market flexibility: panel evidence based on survey data. *European Economic Review* 49: 1225–59.

Djankov, S., Ganser, T., McLiesh, C., Ramalho, R. and Shleifer, A. (2010) The effect of corporate taxes on investment and entrepreneurship. *American Economic Journal: Macroeconomics* 2(3): 31–64.

Domar, E. and Musgrave, R. (1944) Effects of proportional taxes on risk taking. *Quarterly Journal of Economics* 58: 388–422.

Drazen, A. and Easterly, W. (2001) Do crises induce reforms? Some empirical tests of conventional wisdom. *Economics and Politics* 13(2): 129–57.

Easterly, W. (2008) Globalization. *The New Palgrave Dictionary of Economics*, 2nd edn (ed. S. N. Durlauf and L. E. Blume). Palgrave Macmillan.

Easterly, W. and Rebelo, S. (1993) Marginal income tax rates and economic growth in developing countries. *European Economic Review*, 37: 409–17.

Engen, E. M. and Skinner, J. (1996) Taxation and economic growth. *National Tax Journal* 49: 617–42.

Erken, H., Donselaar, P. and Thurik, R. (2008) Total factor productivity and the role of entrepreneurship. Jena Economic Research Papers 2008-019.

Folster, S. and Henrekson, M. (2000) Growth effects of government expenditure and taxation in rich countries. Stockholm School of Economics Working Paper 391.

Friedman, M. (1953) The methodology of positive economics. (Reprinted as Chapter 7 in *The Philosophy of Economics: An Anthology*, 3rd edn (ed. D. M. Hausman). Cambridge University Press, 2008.)

Frontier Economics (2012) The impact of regulation on growth. Report prepared for the Department of Business, Innovation and Skills, BIS/12/821 (www.gov.uk/government/publications/).

Gentry, W. M. and Hubbard, R. G. (2000) Tax policy and entrepreneurial entry. *American Economic Review* 90(2): 283–87.

Gentry, W. M. and Hubbard, R. G. (2004) Success taxes, entrepreneurial entry, and innovation. NBER Working Papers 10551. National Bureau of Economic Research.

Gompers, P. A. and Lerner, J. (1999) What drives venture capital fundraising? NBER Working Papers 6906. National Bureau of Economic Research.

Hansson, P. and Henrekson, M. (1994) A new framework for testing the effect of government spending on growth and productivity. *Public Choice* 81: 381–401.

Hessels, J. and van Stel, A. (2011) Entrepreneurship, export orientation, and economic growth. *Small Business Economics* 37: 255–68.

Heston, A., Summers, R. and Aten, B. (2002) Penn World Table Version 6.1, Center for International Comparisons at the University of Pennsylvania (CICUP).

Hopenhayn, H. and Rogerson, R. (1993) Job turnover and policy evaluation: a general equilibrium analysis. *Journal of Political Economy* 101: 915–38.

Inklaar, R. and Timmer, M. (2008) Accounting for growth in retail trade: an international productivity comparison. *Journal of Productivity Analysis* 29(1): 23–31.

Kirzner, I. M. (1997) Entrepreneurial discovery and the competitive market process: an Austrian approach. *Journal of Economic Literature* 35: 60–85.

Koeniger, W. (2005) Dismissal costs and innovation. *Economics Letters* 88(1): 79–85.

Koester, R. and Kormendi, R. (1989) Taxation, aggregate activity and economic growth: cross-country evidence on some supply-side hypotheses. *Economic Inquiry* 27: 367–86.

Lazear, E. (1990) Job security provisions and employment. *Quarterly Journal of Economics* 105: 699–726.

Leach, G. (2003) *The Negative Impact of Taxation on Economic Growth*. London: Reform.

Leamer, E. E. (1983) Let's take the con out of econometrics. *American Economic Review* 73: 31–43.

Lee, Y. and Gordon, R. H. (2005) Tax structure and economic growth. *Journal of Public Economics* 89: 1027–43.

Leibfritz, W., Thornton, J. and Bibbee, A. (1997) Taxation and economic performance. OECD Working Paper 176.

Leigh, P. and Schembri, M. (2004) Instrumental variables technique: cigarette price provided better estimate of effects of smoking on SF-12. *Journal of Clinical Epidemiology* 57: 284–93.

Levine, R. and Renelt, D. (1992) A sensitivity analysis of cross-country growth models. *American Economic Review* 82: 942–63.

Levine, R. and Zervos, S. J. (1993) What we have learned about policy and growth from cross-country regressions? *American Economic Review* 83: 426–30.

Loayza, N. and Soto, R. (2002) The sources of economic growth: an overview. In *Economic Growth: Sources, Trends, and Cycles* (ed. N. Loayza and R. Soto). Santiago: Central Bank of Chile.

Lucas, R. E. (1990) Supply-side economics: an analytical review. *Oxford Economic Papers* 42(2): 293–316.

Meenagh, D., Minford, P. and Wang, J. (2007) Growth and relative living standards – testing barriers to riches on post-war panel data. CEPR Discussion Papers 6288.

Meenagh, D., Minford, P., Nowell, E. and Sofat, P. (2010) Can a real business cycle model without price and wage stickiness explain UK real exchange rate behaviour? *Journal of International Money and Finance* 29: 1131–50.

Millan, A., Millan, J. M., Roman, C. and van Stel, A. (2013) How does employment protection legislation influence hiring and firing decisions by the smallest firms? *Economics Letters* 121(3).

Minford, L. (2015a) The macroeconomic effects of UK tax, regulation and R&D subsidies: testing endogenous growth hypotheses in an open economy DSGE model. PhD thesis, Cardiff University.

Minford, L. (2015b) Tax, regulation and economic growth: a case study of the UK. Cardiff University Working Papers in Economics, E2105/16, Cardiff Business School, Cardiff University.

Minford, P. and Wang, J. (2011) Public spending, taxation and economic growth – the evidence. In *Sharper Axes, Lower Taxes* (ed. P. Booth), pp. 31–44. Hobart Paperback 38. London: Institute of Economic Affairs.

Mortensen, D. T. and Pissarides, C. A. (1994) Job creation and job destruction in the theory of unemployment. *Review of Economic Studies* 61(3): 397–415.

Murray, M. P. (2006) Avoiding invalid instruments and coping with weak instruments. *Journal of Economic Perspectives* 20(4): 111–32.

Myles, G. D. (2009a) Economic growth and the role of taxation – aggregate data. OECD Economics Department Working Papers 714.

Myles, G. D. (2009b) Economic growth and the role of taxation – disaggregate data. OECD Economics Department Working Papers 715.

Nickell, S. and Layard, R. (1999) Labor market institutions and economic performance. In *Handbook of Labor Economics* (ed. O. Ashenfelter and D. Card). North Holland.

OECD (2004) *OECD Employment Outlook*. Paris: OECD.

Parker, S. C. (1996) A time series model under uncertainty. *Economica* 63: 459–75.

Robson, M. T. (1998) The rise in self employment amongst UK males. *Small Business Economics* 65: 757–73.

Saint-Paul, G. (2002) Employment protection, international specialization, and innovation. *European Economic Review* 46(2): 375–95.

Sala-i-Martin, X. (1994) Cross-sectional regression and the empirics of economic growth. *European Economic Review* 38: 739–47.

Sala-i-Martin, X., Doppelhofer, G. and Miller, R. I. (2004) Determinants of longterm growth: a Bayesian averaging of classical estimates (BACE) approach. *American Economic Review* 94: 813–35.

Slemrod, J. (1995) What do cross-country studies teach about government involvement, prosperity, and economic growth? *Brookings Papers on Economic Activity* 1995(2): 373–431.

Smith, A. (1993) Estimating nonlinear time-series models using simulated vector autoregressions. *Journal of Applied Econometrics* 8: S63–S84.

Solow, R. M. (1956) A contribution to the theory of economic growth. *Quarterly Journal of Economics* 70(1): 65–94.

Solow, R. (1994) Perspectives on growth theory. *Journal of Economic Perspectives* 8(1): 45–54.

Van Stel, A. and Thurik, R. (2007) The effect of business regulations on nascent and young business entrepreneurship. *Small Business Economics* 28(2).

Wennekers, S. and Thurik, R. (1999) Linking entrepreneurship and economic growth. *Small Business Economics* 13(1): 27–55.

PART 3

DESIGNING A NEW TAX SYSTEM

9 THE PRINCIPLES OF A 'GOOD' TAX SYSTEM

Rory Meakin

L'art de l'imposition consiste à plumer l'oie pour obtenir le plus possible de plumes avec le moins possible de cris[1]

Jean-Baptiste Colbert,
finance minister to the French king, Louis XIV

Classical maxims of taxation

Jean-Baptiste Colbert probably meant his famous seventeenth-century maxim on the art of taxation to mean that a tax system ought to raise as much money as possible without people noticing. That is certainly not how a good tax system should operate. But while a good tax system should not attempt to evade taxpayers' notice, it should try to do its job of confiscating money with as little pain as possible for taxpayers and the wider economy. A century later, in 1776, Adam Smith listed four maxims of tax systems which have largely stood the test of time: proportionality, certainty, convenience and efficiency.

Proportionality Subjects should 'contribute towards the support of the government, as nearly as possible, in proportion to

---

1   In English, 'the art of taxation consists in so plucking the goose as to obtain the largest possible amount of feathers with the smallest possible amount of hissing.'

their respective abilities: that is, in proportion to the revenue which they respectively enjoy under the protection of the state' (Smith 1776: 639).

Certainty   Tax should be 'certain, and not arbitrary. The time of payment, the manner of payment, the quantity to be paid, ought all to be clear and plain to the contributor, and to every other person.' Smith was careful to note the risks involved with giving inspectors discretion and his warning about the dangers of uncertainty chime presciently with recent public disquiet about taxes due and payable, especially under Britain's complex corporate tax code.

Convenience   Tax should be 'levied at the time, or in the manner, in which it is most likely to be convenient for the contributor to pay it.' For example, he suggests that tax on rents should be payable 'at the same term at which such rents are usually paid, is levied at the time when it is most likely to be convenient for the contributor to pay; or, when he is most likely to have wherewithal to pay' (Smith 1776: 640).

Efficiency   Tax should be 'so contrived as both to take out and to keep out of the pockets of the people as little as possible over and above what it brings into the public treasury of the state' (Smith 1776: 640). Smith lists four reasons why taxes can be inefficient: administration, tax wedge, costs associated with evasion and compliance burdens.

Bringing Adam Smith up to date

As Mirrlees et al. (2011) noted in *Tax by Design*, these four maxims are almost truisms, not least because they 'may command near-universal support' (p. 22). It is hard to imagine many objecting to the latter three, but many do reject proportionate tax in favour of progressive tax rates. Some objections to proportionality rest on a theoretical basis that, because the utility of income falls as income rises, a bigger proportional monetary sacrifice by a richer person might involve the same sacrifice of utility.

In the context of a progressive system, Mirrlees et al. assumed that the particular distributional outcomes were given and suggested four objectives insofar as other aspects of the tax system were concerned:

- To minimise negative effects on welfare and economic efficiency.
- To minimise administration and compliance costs.
- To maximise fairness other than in a distributional sense (that is, fairness of procedure, avoidance of discrimination and meeting legitimate expectations).
- To maximise transparency: an understandable system is preferable to one that taxes by 'stealth'.

To achieve these objectives, they suggest that simple, neutral and stable systems will perform more effectively than complex, biased and fickle ones.

Mankiw et al. (2009) expanded on Smith's maxims, proposing eight additional principles from the optimal taxation economics literature. Some of the more important ones are listed below.

Optimal margin distributions

Higher marginal rates are less damaging when the rise in marginal rates affects fewer people at the margin and more people infra-marginally. For example, the 40 per cent tax rate is now the marginal rate paid by about 4.5 million people, more than doubling from the 2.1 million who paid the 40 per cent tax rate in 1997. This is more damaging than, for example, a tax system where a smaller number paid 40 per cent tax at the margin but which had the same average tax take (for example, because of higher rates further down the income scale).

Optimal marginal rates could decline at high incomes

Mankiw et al. summarise the argument from Mirrlees by using the following example: 'Suppose there is a positive marginal tax rate on the individual earning the top income in an economy, and suppose that income is y. The positive marginal tax rate has a discouraging effect on the individual's effort, generating an efficiency cost. If the marginal tax rate on that earner was reduced to zero for any income beyond y, then the same amount of revenue would be collected and the efficiency costs would be avoided. Thus, a positive marginal tax on the top earner cannot be optimal' (Mankiw et al. 2009: 7). Given this, it is highly likely that optimal rates (in terms of the trade-off they generate between loss of economic welfare and the tax take) will actually decline with income.

A flat rate tax plus a lump sum transfer could be optimal

The theoretical ideas behind this are complex. However, progressivity could be achieved by having a lump sum transfer to all people (which would be progressive because it would be a bigger proportion of income for the poor) and a flat tax rate (which would avoid the problem of rising marginal rates).

Only final goods should be taxed, and uniformly so

With some exceptions, such as where so-called Pigovian taxes are used to reflect the negative spillover effects of certain economic activities, taxes should not distort consumption patterns. As such, goods and services should be taxed uniformly. We should not try to help the poor by exempting from tax items predominantly bought by the poor because transfer payments and progressive income tax schedules are much more effective and economically efficient ways to help the poor.

Capital income should be untaxed

Because the supply of capital is highly elastic, especially in an open economy, capital taxes discourage investment disproportionately and, consequently, reduce productivity. Furthermore, taxes on capital income tax intermediate inputs (capital) into future outputs, the production and consumption of which are themselves taxed.

Sophistication and redistribution

Additionally, the authors concluded that taxes should be more sophisticated, with separate schedules by age cycles and tags for a range of personal characteristics. They also suggested that optimal redistribution rises with increased income inequality.

Practical impediments to achieving the best tax systems

Clearly, devising an economically 'perfect' tax system is an impossible task, even if the principles can be agreed upon. Many of the principles identified in the literature conflict with others. For example, satisfying the objective of minimising administration and compliance costs would involve a simpler system, partly to ensure that it is more widely understood and therefore reduces welfare losses associated with economic activity discouraged by tax uncertainty. However, more sophisticated systems that adjust marginal rates in order to minimise losses due to the discouragement of work and productivity would make the system more complicated and less simple. It is not clear where the balance should lie between the different principles.

Furthermore, the economic principles enunciated above might conflict with political and ethical principles which might make reform both unpopular and also potentially ineffective. This is especially true if reforms to tax systems effect long-term behavioural changes which are beyond the scope of economic modelling. For example, a reformed tax system which creates a less distortive incentive framework might also be perceived as unfair by enough people to undermine its legitimacy, which could in turn lead to a broader acceptance of avoidance and evasion. This matters because it would mean governments would have to place a heavier burden on compliant taxpayers to raise a given amount of revenue, increasing distortions arising from avoidance and evasion and also increasing the costs of compliance and administration.

A fundamental problem with tax reform is that any reform at all conflicts with the principle of stability. This problem is amplified by a potential conflict with certain measures of fairness when a reform involves an increase in liabilities or an increase in tax rates for particular activities and it is difficult for people engaged in such activities to transfer out of them. So, when a liability is increased, it can impose an effectively retrospective burden on the taxpayer, even if the tax is only due on future activity. For example, a taxpayer may have invested time, effort and money in education, the acquisition of skills or the creation of a business, the fruits of which were only ever expected to be reaped in the future. Even if a reform corrects an existing unfairness, it may create a new one in this way.

More specifically, many tax reform proposals which are based on sound optimal taxation theory appear weaker when they are translated into practical policy recommendations, predominantly due to administrative difficulties in implementation or critiques of the modelling. For example, proposals to reform property taxation by replacing existing taxes with a land value tax are based on strong neutrality and efficiency principles but suffer from substantial practical administrative difficulties. The efficiency rationale supporting a land value tax rests on the exceptionally low level of distortion its implementation should cause. The reason for this is that it should be wholly levied on the economic rent of land ownership, which ought to have a minimal or no impact on landowner incentives to add value by improving property. What can efficiently be taxed is only the value of the land's wilderness state and any potential arising from its proximity to external amenities. In other words, a plot's residual value after any improvements have been subtracted. One problem is designing a system which can value only this component of a property's value without those valuations being affected by improvements that might range from forest-clearing to buildings. Another problem with a land value tax is that it effectively represents a confiscation of an asset class that was lawfully and properly acquired at a price that was based on the assumption that there would be no land value tax levied.

Proposals for a redesign of the tax system

The most significant tax policy reviews have sought to change the tax system so that it more closely adheres to the principles set out in Smith, Mirrlees et al. and Mankiw et al. as discussed above. The two recent significant reviews of the whole UK tax system are those from the TaxPayers' Alliance and the Institute of Directors (*The Single Income Tax*) and the Institute for Fiscal Studies (*Tax by Design*).

In *The Single Income Tax*, Heath et al. (2012) summarised a wide range of justifications for limits on the scope of taxation, offered a rigorous critique of the UK system and then proposed a major reform programme based on ethical constraints, popular opinion and technical efficiency. Relevant literature (from ethics and scripture to polling data and economic theory) was extensively reviewed and reforms to strengthen radically the neutrality and transparency of the system were justified on the grounds of maximising economic welfare, fairness and public legitimacy and confidence in the system through substantial simplification. The question of how these aims might be reconciled when they conflict with each other, however, was not directly addressed, at least theoretically.

Two decisions by Heath et al. reveal the principles behind their proposals. The first, to recommend that tax as a share of national income was reduced to one third, which matched the mean average response in then-recent polling on the desired size of the state, illustrates the importance of public opinion and popular legitimacy of the tax system. Secondly, their rejection of the case to extend the standard rate of VAT to zero and reduced-rate items despite acknowledging its economic efficiency, reveals a scepticism about the net efficiency gains once the cost of ameliorating benefit changes have been accounted for, and also an assessment that the welfare costs arising from direct taxes are a more pressing concern than those from indirect taxes.

Heath et al. recommended a single income tax charged at 30 per cent (hence abolishing national insurance, capital gains tax and corporation tax); devolving tax-raising powers to local authorities; and abolishing stamp duty land tax, stamp duty on shares, inheritance tax and air passenger duty. No significant changes were proposed for other consumption taxes.

The authors did, however, propose substantial changes to local taxation. They recommended devolving more responsibility for tax-raising to local authorities and proposed increasing the share of local government spending in total government spending from its then current level of around a quarter to at least half. They proposed fully devolving business rates, permitting a local sales tax and devolving six percentage points of income tax receipts (from income to labour only) to local authorities. They rejected devolving VAT and income and other taxes on capital income for administrative reasons.

Mirrlees et al. (2011) also proposed substantial reform but said little about the overall burden of tax. They too proposed merging income tax with national insurance and abolishing the £100,000 personal allowance limit, which they described as 'pointless complexities'. They also proposed abolishing stamp duties. However, their approach to addressing the debt–equity bias in corporate finance was to recommend an allowance for corporate equity, an approach also favoured by Keable-Elliott and Papworth (2015).

Mirrlees et al. recommended significant property and consumption tax reforms. Beyond abolishing stamp duty, they called for council tax to be replaced by a housing consumption services tax intended to be similar to VAT, applicable to both rented and owner-occupied property. Business rates would be replaced by a land value tax and inheritance tax by a wealth transfer tax. Almost all exempt, reduced and zero-rated items would be subject to VAT, with increases in transfers to protect low-income groups.

While the authors did suggest bold reforms to the two main local taxes – business rates and council tax – they did not directly comment on the level or range of taxes which ought to be available to local government, except to note the 'fact that land and property have identifiable and unchangeable geographic locations also makes them natural tax bases for the financing of local government' (Mirrlees et al. 2011: 368).

Perhaps the most fundamental difference between the two proposals was their remits. Mirrlees et al. did not address the size of the spending and tax ambitions of the state and treated them as exogenous. They also were content to recommend reform which implied substantial tax increases for certain groups with reductions for others. Heath et al., however, recommended a level of taxation which allowed substantial cuts in total and avoided tax rises for any substantial group. This difference does not lend itself well to direct comparison of the two approaches to the same problem. However, it does highlight that substantial and meaningful tax reform will always involve political hurdles in the form either of spending cuts to ensure nobody loses, or of tax rises to ensure that spending levels are maintained.

Other simplification proposals

Most other reform proposals have broadly echoed the approach of either combining a reduction in the tax share of national income with a substantial simplification of rates, thresholds and bases (as in Heath et al.) or have proposed pursuing the twin aims of simplification and realignment of tax with economic principles as recommended by Mirrlees et al.

Bourne (2014: 9) recommended a 'simple, coherent marginal rate structure which is as flat as possible', including national insurance and benefit withdrawal, arguing that 'significantly lower levels of government spending could facilitate substantial marginal tax rate cuts'.

Herring (2015) recommended simplifying taxes which raise less than £5 billion annually by merging them with other taxes or abolishing them while cutting and rationalising operations, rates and thresholds for larger taxes. Measures included alignment of national insurance with income tax (with a view to merger), merging inheritance tax with capital gains tax, abolishing the additional income tax rate (currently 45 per cent) and allowing trading companies to become tax transparent on a similar basis to the US 'S-corporations' regime.

Proposals for a tax system to promote growth

Of course, the proposals discussed above would have a side-effect of promoting growth. However, some discussions of the tax system have considered growth as the first-order reason for reform. In *Tax Policy Reform and Economic Growth*, the OECD

(2010) recommended broadening tax bases of both consumption and income taxes. It regarded recurrent taxes on immovable property (i.e. not taxes on property transfer) as the least damaging tax. This was followed by consumption taxes as the next least damaging, personal income taxes and then corporate income taxes. Inheritance taxes were also described as having low negative incentive effects, partly because a large fraction of inheritances are unplanned. The OECD also suggest grouping reforms together as linked packages rather than isolated proposals can help overcome objections.

Saatchi (2014), however, recommended a move away from neutrality by abolishing corporation tax for small companies and capital gains tax for investors in small companies. The proposal carries substantial risks of avoidance and distortions but Saatchi justifies them on the grounds of the reduced administrative costs, correction of existing regulatory distortions against small companies, labour and capital responsiveness to lower rates and it being only the 'first step' towards a broader reform.

Property and wealth tax reform proposals

Lawton and Reed (2013: 13) conclude: 'it does not appear that housing is particularly undertaxed as an investment in the UK on average, although it is probably undertaxed as a consumption good'. In other words, perhaps the main recurrent housing property tax (council tax) is not too high or should be supplemented with other forms of tax, but stamp duty is too high. The authors suggest that council tax could be either reformed with a new rate structure or replaced with a residential property value tax. They also acknowledged the economic distortion caused by stamp duty land tax but proposed only converting the structure from a slab rate to a marginal rate one (a reform which has since been implemented).

Tax design rules

The primary function of a good tax system should be to raise money for necessary government spending while causing the least damage possible. The secondary function should be to charge people with the spillover costs of their economic activity that they create which would otherwise be borne by others. To meet these objectives, a good tax system should adhere to four rules based on the principles set out by optimal taxation literature.

Tax should be transparent and certain

Transparency and certainty within the tax system requires, in turn, that the following criteria apply.

- There should be a broad understanding of the basic facts of who pays how much and when.
- Rules, thresholds, schedules and rates should be as simple as possible. There should be as few rates and thresholds as possible.
- Tax should be codified so that taxpayers know what is expected and can arrange their affairs accordingly with any ambiguity kept to a minimum.
- A formal tax strategy should be adopted, with changes announced in advance with explanations how each helps implement the strategy or why a breach of the strategy is necessary.

Taxes should be as neutral as possible

Where feasible, this should be achieved by applying the same tax at the same rate to different activities. In special cases, separately designed taxes should attempt to ensure neutrality.

Marginal rates should be low

To minimise disincentives (except for taxes expressly designed to make those involved in economic activity pay the external costs caused by that activity) tax rates should be comfortably on the left slope of relevant Laffer curves – in other words set so that any losses in revenue resulting from reduced economic growth are relatively low.

Pigovian taxes

Taxes designed to charge people for the costs that their activities impose on others should be set at a level to cover those costs alone at the margin. They should not be used to 'punish' particular activities or to raise revenue that goes beyond the revenue that would be raised from setting the taxes at the level necessary to reflect the external costs of the activity.

These design rules are usually complementary. Simpler tax systems are usually also less distortionary, more administratively efficient and more neutral. However, sometimes the rules will conflict. When conflicts arise, the rules should normally be applied in the order given. Transparency should normally take precedence over neutrality, which should in turn be favoured over efficiency. This is because government should not, as a matter of principle, fail to be as open as it can reasonably be to its citizens about the money it takes from them. Tax is morally problematic enough when applied honestly and transparently (see Butler in Heath et al. 2012: 79–87). These moral problems are exacerbated the more that tax is opaque and citizens do not know how money is taken, and how much is taken.

There is also a practical objection to sacrificing transparency for efficiency. It is difficult to know what the effects are of the uncertainty, suspicion and mistrust that can arise under a system that is not sufficiently transparent to gain widespread legitimacy. The more opaque a tax system is, the less likely people are to be sure that everyone is paying a fair share of the burden, which, in turn, may lead people to be more inclined to avoid or evade their own taxes so that a culture of avoidance rather than compliance develops. This can be exacerbated by inaccurate media reports that result from journalists misunderstanding the system.

Whether efficiency or neutrality should take precedence is less clear. Neutrality may imply a single rate across a range of activities – or across different products in the case of a consumption tax. However, there is a different response of demand to changes in price across different products. In theory, taxes should be lower on a product if the change in demand caused by the tax is greater. However, varying tax rates in this way would breach the transparency and neutrality rules.

Normally, neutrality should be preferred over efficiency because a neutrality rule is more realistically achievable and offers more certainty. There may be cases, however, where the economic inefficiency caused by tax neutrality is so great that it outweighs the normal preference for neutrality. By way of example, where capital is highly mobile, a tax on the foreign earnings of non-domiciled individuals (who are exempt from such a tax) may cause such individuals to leave the country and actually reduce tax revenues. The exemption breaches the neutrality rule, both between domiciled and non-domiciled taxpayers, and between foreign and domestic income of non-domiciled taxpayers. But such a breach may be preferable to the disproportionate breach of the efficiency principle that would arise from taxing such earnings.

A Pigovian tax designed to deal with negative spillovers becomes arbitrary and distortionary to the extent to which the tax exceeds external costs of the relevant economic activity. In some cases, it is possible for a tax on a product or activity that only reflects external costs to be arbitrary and distortionary, too. This is especially the case if an activity is taxed but close substitutes or those that have similar social costs are not. For example, a tax on fizzy drinks containing sugars that is not applied to 'smoothies' or other foods containing high levels of sugar would certainly be arbitrary and, potentially, distortionary (because people may switch to smoothies only for tax reasons even though they prefer fizzy drinks which might have the same level of social costs attached). The administrative costs of the tax, together with the welfare cost to consumers who switch to the 'second best' substitute, could outweigh the welfare gains associated with the reduction of excess consumption by those whose consumption is discouraged but who do not switch to substitutes.

Tax design rules to disregard

Sin taxes

Taxes on activities that impose costs on others can be justified on the basis of maximising efficiency and ensuring that the full costs of economic activities are incurred by those undertake those activities. They also reduce welfare losses insofar as they allow damaging taxes to be reduced. Sin taxes simply levied on activities of which other people disapprove fail to meet these criteria. Alcohol and tobacco duties offer an example of the line between a sin tax and a 'Pigovian' tax to reflect external costs. In a country in which the treatment for conditions associated with consumption of the products is socialised, the extent to which a duty reflects that cost (and funds the treatment) makes it a Pigovian tax. However, the extent to which the duties exceed the external costs defines them either as an arbitrary consumption tax for raising revenue, or as a sin tax to compel people to change their behaviour. As it happens, individuals have very different capacities to consume alcohol and tobacco with differing degrees of harm, which means that the same tax can operate effectively as a Pigovian tax for some but wholly or largely as a sin tax for others. Of course, it is not realistic to design the tax system to avoid this problem.

Fairness

A good tax system should operate fairly in many ways. However, there is no sense of fairness in itself which does not arise from other principles and rules, such as economic efficiency, neutrality and the rule of proportionality described by Smith. In so far as 'fairness' involves playing by the rules and following established principles (the traditional meaning of the word), the principle should be embedded in any tax system that has the characteristics described above. However, if we take fairness to mean that the result of the tax system should produce a particular distribution of incomes that we regard as 'fair', the concept takes on a wholly subjective and unworkable meaning. No specific usefully definition of 'fair' will ever gain full agreement from more than a tiny number of people.

Progressivity

There is no intrinsic merit in the progressiveness of a tax system. A good tax system that aims to be neutral, economically efficient, transparent and proportionate may exhibit some progressivity. But how successfully a tax system helps the poor (or avoids further impoverishing them) should not be judged by how relatively damaging it is to the rich by comparison with them. More so than the rich or people on middle incomes, the poor are likely to become unemployed if the tax system does not nurture growth and enterprise. The poor benefit substantially and often disproportionately from strong economic growth, low unemployment, high productivity and high wages. How a tax system best supports these aims, particularly over the long term, should therefore be reflected in an assessment of how successfully a tax system treats the poor. We should not just consider the first-round effects of taxing rich people proportionately more than poor people.

10 WHAT SHOULD A GOOD TAX SYSTEM LOOK LIKE?

Rory Meakin

The previous chapter reviewed the principles that underpin a good tax system, the practical impediments that might arise and those principles that can be disregarded. We now examine the kind of tax system that the application of the principles we have discussed might produce. We consider taxes on income, consumption and wealth, and then corporate and local taxes. Finally, we list the 'tax death-row' of the current system – that is, those existing taxes that should have no place in a good tax system.

Tax on income

The evidence suggests that flatter rates of income tax are more efficient. A single rate of income tax across all income types would make a tax system transparent, neutral and less distortive. The proposals advanced by Heath et al. (2012) for a single income tax at a single rate, which would operate as the existing income tax does on self-assessed earnings and pay-as-you-earn income but through a new administrative regime for income from the corporate sector, offer the most compelling reform programme for taxes on income.

The taxes considered to be income taxes by the authors include both employee and employer national insurance as well as corporation tax[1] and capital gains tax, which is correctly

---

1   See the section on corporate taxes for further discussion of employer's national insurance and corporation tax.

identified as a duplicated tax on the increase in the net present value of future expected income from an asset.[2]

The two key features of the proposal were, firstly, a single tax on all income types, and, secondly, a single rate of tax, often referred to as a 'flat' rate. The benefit of a single rate is the neutrality and simplicity it offers. As well as the obvious consequence of having only one tax rate to remember and calculate, by removing incentives for taxpayers to shift earnings from one type to another it also eliminates the need for much of the monitoring, anti-avoidance measures and compliance mechanisms involved with policing the distinctions inherent within the system. Deciding how to receive and distribute income, and whether to structure it in the form of employment, self-employment, dividends, share buy-backs, contingent loan interest or personal service companies should become purely commercial ones, undertaken only for reasons of efficiency and governance.

The obvious break with the single rate lies in the personal allowance or tax-free income. Tax systems have one for two main reasons. Firstly, they remove the need to administer tax on the lowest incomes which yield little revenue. Secondly, they remove income tax from those on the lowest incomes, reducing any requirement for benefit payments to be made to the same taxpayer. This further reduces administration costs and improves work incentives by making the personal financial benefit of work more transparent. The level of the tax-free allowance should be set in tandem with appropriate features of the benefit system to minimise opacity and inefficiency in the interaction between the systems.

---

2   Sometimes, income is disguised as capital gain, in which case, the capital gains tax is an attempt to tax income that might otherwise go untaxed (the solution to this problem is to reform income tax). More often, capital gains arise from shares rising in value either because investors expect higher future profits or because companies have retained profits for future investment. In these circumstances, the profits will eventually be taxed when they are distributed and a tax on the increase in the value of the share arising from the retention of profits or from higher expected future profits is, in effect, a double tax.

National insurance

National insurance operates as little more than a secondary income tax (Mirrlees et al. 2011). It is now almost identical in principle to income tax but unacceptably costly and opaque and wholly removed from its original function as a compulsory insurance scheme. A genuinely contributory social insurance system may offer some political-economy benefits of allowing policymakers to resist pressure to increase compulsory benefit levels (and therefore taxation) above their optimal levels, but it is unclear why those on higher incomes ought to be compelled to purchase more expensive/generous insurance or why that would not be best arranged by compelling high earners to purchase such cover directly rather than administering it through the tax and benefits systems. Whether we should revive a genuine contributory social insurance system is a separate matter. However, we currently do not have one and the design of the tax system should reflect that.

Other taxes which apply to income should also be abolished and incorporated into a tax on income along the lines of the Heath et al. proposals, including corporation tax,[3] stamp duties on shares and property purchases (which are transaction taxes but can be seen as an advanced tax on the present value of expected future income from assets), and capital gains tax (which, similarly, represents an advanced tax on the increase in the present value of expected future income from an asset).

Estate and gift taxes

Inheritance tax, which has the nomenclature of an income tax but operates as an estate tax on certain items, should also be either scrapped altogether or merged into income tax, depending

---

3   See the section on corporate taxes for further discussion.

on whether the system views bequests from the perspective of the heir or the deceased.

If viewed from the perspective of the deceased, a bequest can be seen simply as a gift. When someone earns money, tax is normally paid on that income and then again on consumption when it is spent. A tax on bequests breaches the neutrality principle because money spent by an heir is subject to inheritance tax as well as to consumption taxes. It therefore distorts consumption patterns away from saving for future consumption by heirs in favour of immediate or sooner consumption by the benefactor. For example, parents might choose to spend money now buying private education to realise the full value of the assets they have instead of saving them and bequeathing the value less the deduction to pay for the inheritance tax liability.

Viewed from the perspective of the heir, however, an inheritance can be seen as income that would be tax-free if it were not subject to income tax or an equivalent inheritance tax. It therefore breaches the neutrality principle and, perhaps marginally, the transparency principle to exempt bequests from tax by introducing separate rules for different types of income. The low rates principle is also breached, because revenue forgone from an exemption on bequests leads to higher rates for other taxes. Taxing bequests only, however, might open up a breach in the neutrality principle due to the exempt status of gifts made before the benefactor dies if these are untaxed. This then leads to the question of how to treat gifts.

Most countries do not tax gifts. The UK did, between 1975 and 1986, when the 'capital transfer tax' replaced the estates tax and then was itself replaced by inheritance tax (Mirrlees et al. 2011). Practical difficulties involved with monitoring transfers of value, especially between family members, go some way to explaining why the tax did not last long. There is a strong case to be made that a good tax system will subject all gifts, including bequests, to income tax on the recipient, because this approach is transparent, neutral and lowers marginal rates. If one does not regard bequests as income in the proper sense of the word (but a voluntary transfer from one person to another), it could also be argued that exempting all gifts, including bequests, is more transparent and neutral. If this debate cannot be resolved, it could be argued that Smith's principles of convenience and efficiency support exemption of bequests and gifts from tax on the ground that it is inconvenient for families dealing with death to be concerned with tax (which may partly explain why inheritance tax is so unpopular), and the administrative effort required by extending tax to bequests and lifetime gifts. Furthermore, the taxation of bequests and gifts can often be avoided in complex ways which make the tax system less efficient and less transparent.

Separate taxes with additional rules, thresholds, exemptions, allowances and rates for such gifts, however, cannot form a part of a good tax system.

Tax on consumption

Consumption taxes are less distortionary when broad-based. The evidence suggests that distortions can be reduced more efficiently by broadening the tax base for consumption taxes and, if necessary, increasing transfers to poor families to maintain their real incomes as recommended by Mirrlees et al. (2011). As well as reducing overall levels of distortion, the shift would make the tax system more transparent in how it distorts earnings and consumption patterns, strengthening transparency, neutrality and efficiency in the system.

At higher rates, VAT seems likely to be more efficient than a sales tax, which is likely to explain why economies rarely implement sales taxes above, or VAT below, rates of 10 per cent. Sales taxes impose a lighter total compliance burden on businesses because they are levied only on the final product, whereas VAT is applied at every stage in a product's production. A sales tax gives retailers greater incentives to evade the charge, because retailers are liable for the whole amount, whereas under VAT retailers are only liable for their added value. To avoid distortions and inefficiencies created by greater evasion, a good tax system should therefore prefer a VAT to a sales tax if the revenue requirements mean that the rates need to be high. Policymakers should assess the trade-off between evasion and compliance burdens and select a sales tax or VAT accordingly.

Reduced rates, exemptions and housing

To better adhere to the neutrality and transparency principles, almost all exemptions and all reduced rates for VAT should be abolished.[4] But new dwelling construction, repairs and maintenance, and rents should not be subject to VAT. Instead, these items should be captured along with the consumption value of owner-occupied housing with a housing consumption tax which should be set at the same rate as the standard VAT rate and should aim to mimic VAT.

A system such as this this operated in the form of domestic rates until its abolition in 1990, when it was replaced by the community charge ('poll tax') and then council tax. The rates were intended to be reassessed frequently but, in practice, reviews were usually long delayed, which led to even stronger pressure to resist reviews as the changes in particular households' tax rates that the review would lead to would be so great. This distorted spatial patterns of housing consumption and opened a gap in the level of taxation on housing versus other consumption. To avoid repeating this problem, three design features should be implemented:

---

4   Including food, medicine, domestic fuel and children's clothing.

- Assessed rents should be automatically increased annually in line with a local rent index.
- Rent reassessments should be carried out at a fixed frequency, perhaps every four years.
- Rent reassessments should be staggered, ideally randomly but it may by more convenient to reassess whole streets, electoral wards or even local authorities in the same year for administrative efficiency reasons.

Then a tax should be charged on the assessed rental value of the house at a rate equal to the rate of VAT.

Financial services

Many financial services are currently not taxed, in part because EU law prohibits the use of VAT. But it is also because financial services do not operate in a way that allows for a VAT or sales tax to be applied easily (Mirrlees et al. 2011). Financial institutions sometimes charge an explicit fee for their services, but often the fees are hidden in a combination of deposit interest rates on bank accounts which do not fully compensate for the use and risk of capital, and lending rates which charge more than a normal rate of return would demand. With regard to insurance products, an insurance premium (say for house contents insurance) does not represent the value added to the customer of the policy because the pool of customers receive a large proportion of their premiums back in the form of claims – thus the real value added of the policy is the premium less the 'expected value' of the claims at the beginning of the policy year. This is a sum which can be calculated in theory but not in practice.

However, this exemption of financial services breaches the neutrality principle and, in the case of the insurance premium tax charged on insurance products, it also breaches the transparency principle.

Two main approaches to dealing with this problem were identified by Mirrlees et al. (2011). One is to apply a VAT to the sum of wages and profits paid by providers of these services on the grounds that wages and profits approximate to the value added by the products. The second approach, which could be applied to banking services, involves a cash flow tax in which deposits, loan repayments, interest charged and other charges are taxed but withdrawals, interest paid and loans and deductible. This approach could be simplified by applying it only to retail transactions, which would enhance overall neutrality by keeping intermediary factors of production untaxed.

Pigovian taxes

Pigovian taxes ought to be levied to reflect the known and direct costs which consumption of a particular product imposes on others. To the extent that these costs are uncertain and indirect, Pigovian taxes should be reduced. They should also be reduced by the extent to which other externalities are not reflected in the tax system, to avoid creating new distortions by arbitrary and selective treatment of externalities. For example, if there is an externality arising from the consumption of fuel oil for central heating in homes and yet domestic gas consumption is untaxed, taxing fuel oil and not gas would lead people to choose the latter for tax reasons alone, even if the costs of the former were less.[5]

Fuel and roads

Motoring creates costs for non-motorists, the most significant of which are the local environmental and forecasted climate

---

5 Of course, one of the problems of Pigovian taxes is that the range of imperfect substitutes for any product – as defined, in technical terms, by their cross-price elasticity of demand – is huge. As such, putting together the optimal set of Pigovian taxes is a (literally) impossible job. The best that can be achieved is to rectify some of the more clear and damaging externalities.

change costs of emissions; road congestion to other road users; and costs of road maintenance and construction to taxpayers. The government should therefore continue to levy fuel duty to cover both the cost of carbon emissions, and the cost of road maintenance and congestion relating to the roads that it operates.[6]

The Stern Review (2006) estimated the environmental cost of carbon at $85 per tonne. This equates to about 14 pence per litre of petrol, without adjusting for inflation. This estimate is based on a US Environmental Protection Agency (2016) estimate of 8,887 grams of carbon emissions per US gallon. If we multiply the DECC (2015) assumptions for traded short carbon values in the emissions trading scheme (which reflect the cost of reducing carbon emissions elsewhere) by the emissions factors for petrol, this would imply a carbon tax per litre of 1 penny in 2015, rising to 16 pence in 2030 (both at 2015 prices), when a single global carbon price is scheduled to be operating.

Public sector expenditure on national roads in 2014/15 was £3.7 billion, equivalent to approximately 8 pence per litre of petrol sold. A national fuel duty to account for climate change costs and road spending would therefore be set at up to 24 pence per litre. The arguments for fuel duty to cover the cost of congestion are so weak as to be non-existent when set nationally (Wellings 2012) primarily because congestion is specific to locations and times. This is a problem which can only realistically be addressed using road pricing schemes.

Local road spending adds another £5.5 billion, equivalent to 12 pence per litre of petrol sold, to the total. Local authorities should be given the power to raise their own fuel duty to cover construction and maintenance costs of local roads, local congestion and other external costs such as noise and local air pollution.

---

6   That is, assuming other forms of direct charging for road use and a single carbon tax or cap-and-trade system are not implemented.

It should be noted that the overall level of these motoring taxes is currently substantially above the optimal levels. It has been suggested that road building and climate change costs amount to about 36 pence per litre. These are dependent on the extent to which government finances road building and maintenance, and the accuracy of the climate change estimates, which are taken as given for the purposes of this discussion. Road maintenance costs in some rural areas (where costs are spread across fewer journeys) and in dense, expensive central urban zones (where the congestion and opportunity costs of road space are very high) may be much higher, however.

In contrast to that 36 pence per litre total, fuel duty is currently 58 pence per litre and vehicle excise duty (VED)[7] raises £5.9 billion, equivalent to another 13 pence per litre. This charge is illogical, complicated and unnecessary. There are no external costs reflected in VED on cars that cannot be internalised by fuel duty, and congestion and parking charges. It also represents a regressive barrier to car ownership, effectively using tax to price poor people off the roads instead of low-value journeys, breaching the good tax principles of transparency and neutrality. VED should be abolished, but a replacement tax levied on the heaviest road transport vehicles to reflect estimated additional road maintenance costs which are not covered by fuel duty may be acceptable.

While fuel appears to be substantially overtaxed due to fuel duty, other uses of fuel which create emissions are not overtaxed. For example, not only is there no equivalent duty charged on fuel for domestic heating and cooking, but it is also only subject to a reduced rate of VAT set at 5 per cent, a quarter of the standard

---

7   VED could be justified if the marginal costs of road use are very low and therefore total costs are not covered by levies such as fuel duties. This is only likely to be the case in some areas of the country. If roads were privately managed, for example, in rural areas, an efficient charging system might involve an annual pass for access. However, in a uniform tax-funded system, it is very difficult to justify VED.

20 per cent rate. These differences breach the neutrality principle. A good tax system should treat emissions equally, ideally simplifying taxes (and opaque regulatory quasi-taxes such as renewables obligations) into a single carbon tax or bringing all emissions within a cap-and-trade system.

Gambling, alcohol and tobacco

Gambling, alcohol and tobacco consumption can be thought to impose costs on others, to the extent to which certain services are financed collectively. Medical treatments and the enforcement of law and order attributable to both alcohol and tobacco are not insubstantial and, to the extent that consumption is associated with increased expenditure on law and order and medical treatment, they represent costs to others which have either been externalised by collective financing or were inherently external. There are several problems with attempting to apply Pigovian analysis to taxes on gambling, tobacco and alcohol, however.

Firstly, because people's physiological and behavioural responses to substances varies greatly, so does the extent to which a uniform tax adheres to Pigovian principles rather than being an arbitrary, distortionary tax. In other words, taxes can encourage people who can cope well with gambling, alcohol or tobacco consumption to consume less than optimal quantities, thus harming their quality of life.

Secondly, further distortions are caused by a tax system that does not cover all external costs (and external benefits). Why should smoking be discouraged through the tax system if there are other activities that are not taxed and that lead to problems for which the law may also require collectively financed treatment, such as horse-riding or boxing?

Any assessment of the average external cost imposed on others through alcohol and tobacco consumption should be discounted to reflect both of these conceptual problems before attempting to arrive at an economically efficient tax. In this case, the government would come closer to meeting the principles of transparency and neutrality if alcohol were taxed at a single rate per litre of pure alcohol irrespective of the nature of the drink containing it and gambling and tobacco similarly had their tax structures simplified (ending the distinction between rolling and pipe tobacco, for example). Attempts to focus alcohol taxes on 'problem drinkers', such as by taxing spirits or high strength beer more heavily, will further distort consumption and add complexity and consumers will respond by demanding products just under the thresholds.

It is also worth noting that evidence that price mechanisms can affect problematic behaviour is weak. Manning (1995) found that the 'results indicate that both light and heavy drinkers are much less price elastic than moderate drinkers. Further, we cannot reject the hypothesis that the very heaviest drinkers have perfectly price inelastic demands.'

Given the extent of the discounts necessary to adjust average estimated external costs down to reflect the problems above in order to calculate an economically efficient Pigovian tax, it is likely that the tax may be small. As such, abolishing such taxes altogether may be the best way to meet the principle of efficiency (due to the high costs of collection and compliance relative to low receipts and any benefits from the tax from aligning social costs and benefits of the activity) and the principle of transparency (due to the complexity of maintaining taxes which serve minimum fiscal or Pigovian economic functions), even within a collectively financed medical treatment and law enforcement environment.

Taxes on wealth

The case against taxes on wealth in general is overwhelming because they breach two principles of good tax design. They breach Smith's convenience maxim because they are levied without a flow of cash to finance them. And they breach his efficiency maxim because they are associated with a disproportionately large behavioural response as owners of wealth seek to avoid them. There is also a strong case against wealth taxes due to the distortion they create between consumption and savings (or viewed another way, between consumption now and consumption later). This distortion means that immediate consumption is privileged and saving (and therefore investment) is discouraged, reducing productivity growth.

Consider two individuals who each earn £10,000. The first opts to spend all the money now. The second, meanwhile, opts to save it. A 1 per cent wealth tax would mean the second earner would effectively only receive £9,900 thereby introducing a disincentive against saving money, distorting the decision of when to spend it. If the risk-free interest rate were 3 per cent, this 1 per cent wealth tax would be equivalent to a 33.3 per cent tax on interest. However, investment returns should, in any case, be taxed separately if it is deemed appropriate to tax interest. Tax on interest has the same effect, introducing a distortion between spending now and later by discouraging the latter, although the case for taxing interest is somewhat stronger than taxing capital itself.

Location value tax

One exception, however, is tax that captures the location value of land. If properly constituted, a tax on location value may cause disproportionately little economic damage, because land cannot be hidden or taken overseas to avoid the tax and owners cannot respond to the tax by producing less value in its location – for the reason that they are not responsible for it in the first place. A location value tax involves a tax on the value of land in a given location which is normally calculated on the assumption of the land being in its most valuable permitted use. However, it is a tax on the land value only and not on any associated buildings.

In one sense, implementing a location value tax on land ownership would appear to breach the neutrality principle because of the seemingly arbitrary treatment of different asset classes (land would be treated differently from business capital, for example). However, the overriding economic objective of the neutrality principle is to minimise arbitrary distortions in the economy, because these lead to economic inefficiency. But, given the strong theoretical case that there are minimal such distortions caused by a tax on location value, it seems that the neutrality principle is not strongly engaged here. Given the powerful economic efficiency merits of this tax, a good tax system ought to disregard the formal neutrality objections.

A further objection arises from the fact that the burden of a location value tax falls on the owner of the land at the time when the tax is announced. The value of the land should fall immediately by the discounted present value of the expected future tax payments required under the tax. It is therefore a windfall tax on landowners and amounts to arbitrary and retrospective confiscation of the value of their assets. This would ordinarily constitute an unacceptable obstacle to the design of a good tax system but these objections could be outweighed by the otherwise highly efficient nature of the tax together with some carefully designed transitional measures. The loss of value to landowners who have done little to improve their property except wait while the amenities and services provided by others have spilled over into the value of their land, pushing up its value, may not command widespread sympathy. But breaching the neutrality principle in this way does not seem fair to those whose investments – and the sacrifices of deferred consumption – were used to buy land rather than other asset classes. And some portion of the location value is likely to have been bought with money earned from labour or other investments. Finally, in a property market where many properties are purchased with mortgages, a tax could push many landowners into negative equity, causing some combination of property market ossification as owners become unable to move and financial market distress as owners default on debts. These effects could cause problems in the wider economy.

Because the present value of a cash flow in the future is lower than one now, and lower still for one even further into the future, the extent to which the tax represents a windfall charge on the asset's value at the time of the announcement is governed by the length of the delay until its implementation. A delayed and possibly phased introduction should be considered to reduce the impact on financial markets and minimise potential immobility from negative equity. This, along with two other factors should reduce the extent of the regrettable windfall tax element of the charge.

The first is the fact that location value of land is almost always also owned by the same agent who owns the value of the improvement to the land and usually any structures on it. This of course does not reduce the extent of that on the value of the location that would be expropriated, but it would reduce the extent of it measured against the whole value of the property. The second is that the tax should not be designed to appropriate 100 per cent of the location value, both to ensure a margin of error so that it does not exceed 100 per cent and also to leave some private incentive for the landowner to navigate any regulatory or bureaucratic obstacles such as land use planning which may otherwise impede more efficient land use changes.

Another transitional option could be that location value tax might replace the community infrastructure levy and obligations such as affordable housing requirements made under section 106 of the Town and Country Planning Act 1990. Abolishing these two policies would constitute a windfall gain to landowners which would counteract the windfall loss imposed by a location value tax. A government might therefore wish to consider making properties which would have been subject to these charges immediately liable for the location value tax while delaying its introduction on other properties. The same principle also applies to business rates and council tax, so governments might also wish to delay their abolition until they introduce the location value tax.

As long as there are more economically damaging taxes which could be reduced – including on property – the objective of a location value tax should be to extract as much of the economic rent from land ownership as possible. Implicit in this condition is the assumption that the tax can reduce landowners' incentives to apply for planning permission to develop land and that distortions caused by blunting this profit signal should be incorporated into analysis of its relative harm compared with other taxes. However, land-use planning restrictions currently depress the value of agricultural land by as much as 99 per cent. A location value tax would mean that the tax authority would benefit when the planning authority granted permission which increased the value of land. If the taxes accrue to the same authority which decides planning policy, it could improve the incentive structure faced by decision-makers in planning authorities, leading to less inefficient land-use planning policies.

A detailed feasibility study ought to be commissioned, but there does not seem to be any fundamental reason why a location value tax could not be implemented by extending the process used by the Valuation Office Agency for business rates.

National accounts valued total housing rental values at £226 billion in 2014, comprising £59 billion of actual rental payments and £166 billion of imputed values for owner-occupied housing. If we assume that one-third of this amount is the value of the location, this equates to an annual location value of housing at £74 billion. A tax that captured 75 per cent of that could raise £56 billion. Non-domestic property has been valued at £1.9 trillion. Assuming a location value yield of 5 per cent and a variety of location value assumptions depending on the type of property, perhaps £27 billion might be raised from offices, retail, infrastructure and other non-domestic property.

Similarly, the ONS estimated average farm rental values at £171 per hectare in 2013/14. Assuming that 75 per cent of that total represents the location (and unimproved land) value, and that a tax might collect 75 per cent of that, a tax on Britain's 18,456 hectares could yield £1.8 billion. In total, these amount to an estimated £84 billion of revenue that should be substantially less economically damaging than other tax types. Equivalent to 4.6 per cent of GDP, this compares with the £66 billion raised by council tax, business rates and stamp duty land tax in 2014/15.

There would be many practical administrative questions to answer, such as measurement of plots, whether gardens would be assessed separately from land with structures (or permission for them), whether to assess the charge based on an estimate of rental values or sale values, and how to minimise the negative impact on current owners. But its introduction should be considered alongside the array of related taxes which ought to be abolished: business rates; stamp duty land tax; council tax (which in any case should be replaced by a previously discussed simulated extension of VAT to housing); and fiddly local quasi-taxes (the community infrastructure levy and so-called 'affordable housing requirements' and other obligations under 'section 106' of the Town and Country Planning Act 1990).

Corporate tax

The economic literature suggests that, generally, only final goods should be taxed (at the same rate) to avoid distortions in how businesses choose factors of production and in consumption patterns. This supports the principles of transparency and neutrality because a consumption tax on final goods is easier to attribute and is therefore transparent and also more likely to be neutral. Intermediate taxes, therefore, should be abolished. This would include, prima facie, employer's national insurance[8] and business rates.

Commercial property

To the extent to which business rates are a tax on location, they have very low inefficiency costs, for the reasons described in the previous section on wealth taxes. By contrast, to the extent to which they tax improvements or structures that are used for business (e.g. offices, factories, shops, etc.), they represents an arbitrary distortion discouraging the use of property by businesses in the production of goods and services for consumption. Commercial property is consequently underused, reducing productivity (and therefore wages).

It should be noted that we should not argue that commercial and residential property should be taxed the same way in order to achieve neutrality. Commercial property is a factor of production that leads to the production of goods that are then taxed at the consumption stage. A good tax system should seek neutrality in property use by taxing the consumption of residential property (whether rented or imputed from owner occupancy) and by taxing the value of final goods and services consumed which use commercial property in their production.

The distortions created by taxes on intermediate factors of production breach the principles of good tax design in several ways. Beyond the breach of neutrality discussed above, they also constitute an impediment to tax transparency and serve to obfuscate the incidence of who pays how much of which taxes.

Consumers can easily calculate how much VAT they have been charged because VAT is administered with reference to the price of the good or service purchased and the burden falls largely on the consumer. But a consumer is much less able to calculate

---

8   See taxes on income section for further discussion

how much of the purchase price was accounted for by business rates in the various stages of production, for example.

This application of the principles of transparency and neutrality extends beyond property taxation to profit taxes, employer labour taxes and, to some degree, Pigovian taxes.

Corporate profits

The OECD found that corporate income taxes (such as the UK corporation tax) have the most negative impact on economic growth, among consumption taxes, property taxes and income taxes (Arnold 2008). Specifically, corporate income taxes have the following problems:

- They weaken the signal to reallocate resources from low-value activities to high-value activities between different companies and also within the same company by reducing after-tax profits.
- They bias ownership structures in favour of debt capital and against equity capital.
- They distort spending patterns in favour of current expenditure, which is fully tax deductible, and against capital expenditure, which is not (capital allowances partially ameliorate this).
- They discourage investment by reducing retained earnings, which would otherwise be spent on capital investment goods directly by the company or invested with financial intermediaries to the same effect by third parties.

Mirrlees et al. (2011) proposed an allowance for corporate equity (ACE), which would provide companies with an allowance for the normal return on equity investment with the aim of tackling the problems identified above and restricting corporation tax to excess returns, which should disproportionately reduce its negative impact on investment. This approach has been adopted in Italy and was recently recommended by Keable-Elliott and Papworth (2015). While this approach has certain advantages, the measure has flaws which render it an unsatisfactory response to the problems of corporation tax.

The first flaw is that taxation of retained earnings and therefore investment would remain in place, thereby continuing to reduce growth and productivity to some degree leaving marginal rates higher than they might otherwise be. The second flaw is that a breach of the neutrality principle would remain. Debt finance would continue to enjoy a tax advantage over equity finance, high-value activities would still be disadvantaged relative to low-value activities, and capital expenditure would still be disadvantaged relative to current expenditure, with all the inefficiency costs remaining, albeit reduced in scope. But perhaps the most dissatisfying flaw is that the proposal would worsen the overall transparency of the system.

The difficulty of defining profit and attributing it to the right jurisdiction for tax purposes is at the heart of much of the operational dysfunction and public disquiet over corporate tax in recent years. The very existence of corporate income taxes serves to obfuscate the economic functioning of tax to the general public, who, understandably, do not take the time to study tax incidence. The burden can only be borne by some combination of capital, labour or consumers. Corporate income taxes hides this truism by disconnecting the official, legal incidence with the real, economic incidence. This means that many members of the general public struggle to understand its consequences, leading to mistrust of the system and a sense of unfairness.

A much more conceptually satisfying approach to the problem would lie in abolishing tax on corporate income altogether and reforming personal income tax to ensure complete neutrality between all forms of labour and capital income, recommended by Heath et al. (2012). The authors proposed a 'single income tax' with tax on capital income administered at the corporate level in a similar way to PAYE tax on wages (see Heath et al. (2012) for further details).

The debt–equity bias would then be eliminated, along with disadvantages to capital expenditure and high-value activity. The reduction of investment inherent in a tax on retained corporate earnings would also be removed, further enhancing productivity growth.

Employer labour taxes

Similarly, a good tax system would not feature any employer taxes on labour (such as employers' national insurance contributions) for essentially the same reasons: they artificially separate the official, legal incidence of tax from its real, economic incidence, breaching transparency and neutrality principles for no obvious gain. It is likely that taxes on employers worsen economic efficiency by raising the cost of employing labour. While the burden of employer taxes on labour is borne by employees in the long term in the form of lower wages, descriptions of them as employment-reducing 'jobs taxes' are plausible in the short term as wages take time to adjust to changes in employer taxes.

Business Pigovian taxes

A good tax system may, however, allow for Pigovian taxes administered by business when the circumstances are such that charging it to the final value of the consumption is too removed from the external cost which the tax seeks to internalise, or where the administrative costs would be prohibitive.

The general principles of when Pigovian taxes can operate as part of a good tax system are discussed in the section on taxes on consumption. Briefly, they should seek to internalise costs which the activity or consumption creates for third parties, but that this should be discounted to take account of uncertainty in measurement, and the incompleteness of the tax system's Pigovian scope, to avoid creating distortions between consumption where some activities with negative externalities are taxed and others are not.

Adhering to the transparency principle presents a hurdle for Pigovian taxes because separate taxes, rates, rules and thresholds should be avoided where possible. But a further hurdle exists for taxes which are paid by companies. Taxes on intermediate stages of the production chain should be avoided because they breach the transparency principles (because they disconnect legal incidence from economic incidence). However, at least conceptually, an exception could be made for Pigovian taxes because they can be thought of as a charge to reflect the external costs of an activity or mode of production. For example, if it is believed that taxes should be charged to reflect the cost of carbon emissions, this should only be done in respect of those forms of energy generation that emit carbon. So, some producers of energy may pay such a tax and others not, reflecting the different extent to which their methods of production lead to higher carbon emissions.

The bank levy

An example of where a Pigovian approach might be acceptable is in the case of the bank levy, which is a tax on bank liabilities. The bank levy was introduced to compensate taxpayers for the costs to taxpayers involved in bailing out banks considered to be too big to fail. Its function is therefore akin to an insurance premium as much as it is to a Pigovian tax. A bank levy can be justified when taxpayers are exposed to potential costs arising from the inevitability of a bailout due to a combination of their systemic importance to the wider economy and the inadequacy of insolvency laws to ensure orderly failure.

A bank levy's current acceptability, however, does not imply that it ought to be a permanent feature of a good tax system. It can only be part of a good tax system if the regulatory environment is flawed and requires taxpayers to bear risks of bank failure. The current design also fails to reflect the risk profile of the banks concerned. While the size of the balance sheet is loosely linked to the potential size of taxpayers' exposure, it is a crude measure and arguably fails to fully account for risk factors which influence the likelihood of failure. It is beyond the scope of this section to recommend how a closer alignment might operate, but a good tax system should avoid charging a more prudent bank the same levy as a bank with riskier characteristics.

Local taxation

There is a strong link between the efficiency of local government and the extent to which revenues are raised locally. Countries with more devolved government tend to deliver more efficient public services (Gemmell et al. 2013) and have lower levels of spending and taxation (Buser 2011). There are few reasons to suppose that tax systems which are *perfect* for their locations would vary much from place to place, but evidence suggests that those which do not allow for a high degree of local variation tend to be worse than those which do (see Heath et al. (2012), Booth (2015) and Packer and Sinclair (2015) for further discussion and review of the literature).

The overall extent of local taxation should be determined by the scope of local government. Broadly, local spending should be financed by local taxes, so that the mix of local versus national taxes should consequently be determined by the mix of local versus national expenditure.

Some taxes are better suited to local authority control than others. A location value tax could be levied by local authorities, which could then receive all its revenues. This could raise up to 4.6 per cent of national income,[9] compared with the 3.6 per cent raised currently by council tax, business rates and stamp duty land tax combined.

A surcharge on fuel duty may also form part of a good local tax system. Ideally, market-based mechanisms for allocating road space (such as road pricing and better parking charges) would eliminate most of the negative local externalities associated with driving, but in their absence a case can be made for this a local fuel duty (see the consumption taxes section for further discussion).

It is difficult to imagine a value added tax being suitable for devolution to local level because of the fact that production tends to be national and VAT is administered in all parts of the production chain. Potentially, a separate VAT apparatus might be required for each authority, with exempt status for 'exports' and a liability on 'imports' to the local authority area. By contrast, a local sales tax on final consumption values would be much simpler to administer at local level, and they are used in many countries.

Similarly, income tax on labour could be suitable for partial devolution, as recommended by Heath et al. (2012). This allows local authorities to breach the principles of transparency and neutrality which the 'single income tax' proposal would achieve because the rates on capital income and labour income in an authority would no longer be the same if the authority chose to alter the tax rate on labour. The nature of the single income tax proposals regarding capital income

---

9   See the section on wealth taxes for further discussion.

Box 4   Tax death-row

The tax death-row comprises a list of the twenty main taxes which should no longer exist once a good system has been implemented. There is also a brief note explaining why they should be abolished. Some have already been discussed when exploring matters of a good tax system but some are mentioned for the first time.

Tax death-row: existing taxes with no place in a good tax system

Corporation tax	Replace with a tax on corporate income from capital.
Affordable housing and other s106 obligations	Obligations under section 106 of the Town and Country Planning Act 1990, which operate effectively as taxes on property development with some of the cost being borne by land values, should be abolished, albeit with some of its function replaced by a location value tax.
Aggregates levy	This tax on quarrying aggregates exists to reflect the associated externalities but the harm to local environments from quarrying would be better managed by regulation that requires sites are made good after aggregates have been extracted.
Air passenger duty	Fiddly and already partially covered by the EU's emissions trading scheme, flights should be fully brought into the ETS
Alcohol duties	The case for Pigovian tax on alcohol is weak with socialised healthcare provision but becomes almost non-existent in its absence.
Apprentice-ship levy	The apprenticeship levy will makes a badly designed income tax system even worse, introducing new distortions, further opacity and additional complexity. It should be abolished.
Bank surcharge	No principled reason exists to support the bank surcharge on profits. Profitability is a poorer indicator of taxpayer exposure than balance sheets, which the bank levy captures more effectively when a flawed regulatory environment exposes taxpayers to risk of bank failure. It should be abolished.
Business rates	A halfway house between a damaging intermediate tax on commercial property and an efficient tax on location value, business rates should be replaced by a location value tax.
Capital gains tax	Most capital gains represent double taxation on the difference in the present value of expected future income between the dates of purchase and the sale of the asset. This is already effectively taxed and so presents an obstacle to the efficient reallocation of capital assets within the economy.

Climate change levy and renewables obligations	Following the abolition of exemptions on renewable energy sources, the climate change levy now operates as a tax on industrial energy use irrespective of carbon emissions. It should be abolished and replaced with either a comprehensive carbon tax or the full inclusion of emissions into the EU-ETS, which would allow regulatory quasi-taxes such as renewables obligations to be abolished.
Community infrastructure levy	The complex, arbitrary and contentious community infrastructure levy should be abolished, albeit with some of its function replaced by a location value tax.
Corporation tax	Replace with a tax on corporate income from capital.
Council tax	Confused, outdated and unpopular, council tax should be replaced by a location value tax.
Diverted profits tax	This would be defunct when profits are not taxable.
Gambling duties	The case for Pigovian tax on gambling is almost non-existent.
Inheritance tax	There is a coherent, strong case to tax inheritances as part of income in the hands of the recipient, but the case for outright abolition is probably stronger still, for reasons discussed in the section on income tax. There is no case at all for the existing inheritance tax with its poor choice of base (the size of the estate bequeathed) and its substantial and highly distortionary exemptions (such as artworks and agricultural land).
Licence fee	There is no principled case for a tax on the ownership or use of televisions or other broadcasting receiving equipment.
Stamp duty land tax	Similarly, there is no good reason to tax the transactions of properties. This tax artificially depresses property values, discourages investment and distorts the allocation of assets – for example, by discouraging older people from moving to smaller accommodation when they no longer need as much space after their children have left the family home.
Stamp duty on shares	There is no good reason to tax the transactions of shares and this tax artificially depresses equity values, discourages investment and distorts the allocation of assets
Tobacco duties	The case for Pigovian tax on tobacco is weak with socialised healthcare provision but becomes almost non-existent in its absence.
Vehicle excise duty	There are no principled reasons to retain VED on cars, but a per-vehicle tax on heavy transport vehicles to reflect external costs of road maintenance not already covered by fuel duty could be acceptable.

mean that, like VAT, they are administratively unsuitable for devolution.[10]

This breach of neutrality and transparency is unlikely to be necessary with existing local expenditure levels of around 6 per cent of national income because other sources could easily meet that level of expenditure while adhering more closely to the principles of good taxation. It may also be preferable to devolve the revenues (although perhaps not the ability to set the rate, in order to maintain neutrality between types of consumption) from the housing consumption tax proposed in the consumption taxes section.

Though the local variation of income tax is not of itself desirable, the benefits arising from localisation might be greater, especially as it would strengthen the transparency of local government finance. For example, Booth (2015) proposes a substantial and symmetrical devolution of expenditure below a federal British government which would retain control of little more than external affairs, defence, working age welfare and the servicing existing national debt. This would be combined with localisation within the constituent nations of a federal UK. He cites findings from Blöchliger (2013: 4) that demonstrate: 'Doubling sub-central tax or spending shares (e.g. increasing the ratio of sub-central to general government tax revenue from 6 to 12%) is associated with a GDP per capita increase of around 3%.'

The shape of a good tax system

Overall, a good tax system should be radically simpler than the current system, comprising a single income tax at a single rate charged on all income; a single consumption tax with no exempt items; and a location value tax on all land to extract a large proportion of the rent from the unimproved value. There could be

---

10 See Heath et al. (2012), Meakin (2012) and the section on corporate taxes for further discussion.

additional Pigovian taxes limited to internalising external costs, or equivalent rights trading schemes, such as either a carbon tax or an extension of the EU emissions trading scheme; a bank levy; and a local fuel duty. Specific taxes on different types of consumption should be avoided wherever possible, as should different taxes on different types of incomes. Transaction and wealth taxes should be avoided, with the exception of a location value tax.

11 THE FUTURE FOR TAXATION IN THE UK

Rory Meakin

In the previous chapter we looked at how the principles and rules of a good tax system should be applied in practice in different areas of taxation; which taxes ought to be abolished; and then the overall shape of a good tax system. This chapter considers the specific rates necessary to capture a given share of national income and the distribution of the burden by income groups. It will also examine a range of tax administration aspects relating to matters such as the need for a formal tax strategy, annual budgets and monitoring of reliefs and exemptions. The proposals model the effects of introducing the following tax system:

- Heath et al. (2012) style 'single income tax' set at 15 per cent of income above a 2014/15 personal allowance of £10,000.
- VAT set at 12.5 per cent, with most reduced, zero and exempt rates increased to the standard rate.
- A new housing consumption tax on rents and imputed rents to mimic VAT at 12.5 per cent.
- A new location value tax designed to capture an average of 75 per cent of the location value of land ownership.
- Fuel duty retained and set at an average of around half its current rate.
- Bank levy, receipts from the emission trading scheme (ETS), climate change levy and other HMRC taxes left with receipts unchanged but some operational reform.

- Corporation tax, national insurance, capital gains tax, inheritance tax, council tax, business rates, the television licence fee, the apprenticeship levy, stamp duties, alcohol duties, tobacco duties, vehicle excise duty and air passenger duty all abolished.

At these rates, it is estimated that national account taxes would capture around 22.5 per cent of national income at market prices,[1] or around £410 billion in 2014/15.[2] This is roughly equivalent to the top end of the level of government spending that, it has been suggested, might lead to the highest level of economic growth.

Distributional issues

What activities and events will the proposed system tax?

These proposals would lead to one third of revenues being raised from VAT (not including the housing consumption tax) and another third from income tax. Another quarter would be raised by property tax (including a housing consumption tax) with other taxes raising the remaining tenth. This contrasts with the status quo where, in 2014/15, over half of revenues are raised by income taxes with VAT raising one fifth and property taxes one tenth. Other taxes raise the remainder, around a seventh of the total.

As a share of GDP, the proposals represent a substantial cut in income taxes, which would capture an estimated 7.3 per cent of GDP (down from 17.8 per cent under the status quo). Overall, VAT would increase slightly, to 7.2 per cent (from 6.8 per cent). Property tax would rise to 5.6 per cent (from 3.6 per cent). Other taxes would fall to 2.3 per cent (from 4.7 per cent).

---

1 Perhaps around 25 per cent of national income at factor cost.

2 On a static basis; dynamic effects are ignored.

The shift can be characterised as a move from income and arbitrary sin taxes towards heavier property taxes and a broader, flatter VAT. The increase in property tax is substantial. At 3.6 per cent of GDP, the UK already has the highest property tax receipts in the OECD. The proposals involve a substantial reduction in the harmful consumption and transaction elements of property taxes and an elimination of tax on business property. There is, instead, a tax on location value. Overall, this package should substantially improve economic efficiency.

The removal of tax on working capital in the UK corporate sector by abolishing corporation tax and applying tax only to distributed income should also represent a further structural enhancement of the tax system's economic efficiency.

Distributional effects on households by income decile

The proposals represent a substantial tax cut, with national account taxes capturing an estimated 22.5 per cent of GDP (at market prices), down by a third from the current level of 33 per cent. The overall package would be substantially progressive at the lower end of the income distribution but mildly regressive at the upper end. The removal of regressive taxes on property and 'sin' drives the progressiveness of the package at the lower end, but these reforms have less impact at the higher end of the distribution, where the reductions in progressive income taxes are more significant.

Basic static modelling would suggest that the poorest decile would enjoy tax cuts worth 26 per cent of gross income, followed by 19 per cent, 17 per cent and then 13 per cent for the fourth poorest decile before further falling to 7 per cent for the fourth richest decile (see Figure 19 and Table 18). The third richest decile would enjoy a cut of 9 per cent while the richest two deciles would both see their tax cut by 13 per cent of their incomes.

Figure 19 Impact of tax changes by income decile

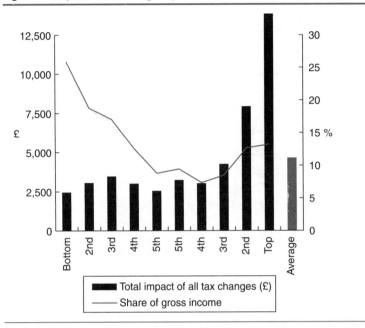

All deciles would enjoy substantial cuts on a static analysis and the overall package is progressive. But it should be noted that such a static analysis is likely to underestimate significantly the extent of progressivity of the reforms. As we noted previously, the structural inefficiencies which would be reduced substantially should have an effect on employment, productivity and wage levels. These effects disproportionately benefit the poor as they are more likely to be at the margins of the labour market in insecure, low-paid employment or unemployed. Moreover, Alloza (2016) recently found that marginal tax rates have a significant effect on the mobility of people through the income deciles, reducing the probability of changing income decile by 0.8 per cent for each percentage point increase in marginal tax rates.

Table 18 Distributional effects data, by household income decile

Distributional effects	Bottom	2nd	3rd	4th	5th	5th	4th	3rd	2nd	Top	Average
Alcohol, tobacco and gambling taxes	499	682	680	598	724	844	731	817	766	898	724
APD, VED and half fuel duty	477	563	614	700	813	980	1,004	1,229	1,299	1,468	915
TV Licence	110	103	112	113	113	117	122	125	133	137	118
Sin taxes removed	1,086	1,348	1,406	1,411	1,650	1,941	1,857	2,171	2,198	2,503	1,757
Share of gross income	11.4%	8.3%	6.9%	5.9%	5.7%	5.7%	4.5%	4.3%	3.5%	2.4%	4.5%
Stamp duty on homes	78	68	61	63	96	106	155	232	353	600	181
Council tax	752	742	823	932	1,003	1,146	1,200	1,317	1,427	1,572	1,091
Business rates	203	219	229	247	282	307	329	381	431	538	317
VAT on rents & imputed rents	–188	–145	–132	–182	–155	–259	–392	–385	–602	–1,710	–415
Location value tax	0	0	0	–1,116	–2,641	–3,125	–4,092	–5,023	–5,953	–9,301	–3,162
Property taxes reformed	845	884	981	–56	–1,416	–1,825	–2,801	–3,478	–4,344	–8,301	–1,989
Share of gross income	8.9%	5.4%	4.8%	–0.2%	–4.9%	–5.3%	–6.8%	–7.0%	–6.9%	–7.9%	–5.1%

Table 18 Continued

Distributional effects	Bottom	2nd	3rd	4th	5th	5th	4th	3rd	2nd	Top	Average
Income tax current bill	226	455	755	1,266	2,132	3,238	4,519	6,104	9,086	20,278	4,806
Income tax reduction	11	23	38	63	107	162	226	305	2,611	6,808	1,035
National insurance	448	663	865	1,196	1,601	2,049	2,661	3,469	4,338	5,725	2,302
Corporation tax	228	321	426	656	848	1,138	1,447	1,902	3,119	7,157	1,724
CGT and inheritance tax	69	66	69	111	135	190	230	303	708	2,070	395
Income taxes cut	756	1,072	1,398	2,026	2,690	3,540	4,565	5,980	10,774	21,759	5,456
Share of gross income	7.9%	6.6%	6.9%	8.5%	9.3%	10.3%	11.1%	12.0%	17.2%	20.8%	13.9%
VAT main rate reduction	488	648	645	747	898	1,050	1,171	1,361	1,616	2,043	1,067
VAT increase on reduced, zero and exempt	-712	-887	-954	-1,115	-1,269	-1,465	-1,760	-1,782	-2,311	-4,161	-1,640
VAT changes net reduction	-224	-239	-309	-367	-371	-415	-589	-421	-695	-2,118	-573
Share of gross income	-2.4%	-1.5%	-1.5%	-1.5%	-1.3%	-1.2%	-1.4%	-0.8%	-1.1%	-2.0%	-1.5%
Total impact of all tax changes (£)	2,463	3,066	3,476	3,014	2,554	3,240	3,032	4,252	7,933	13,844	4,651
Share of gross income	25.9%	18.8%	17.1%	12.6%	8.8%	9.5%	7.4%	8.5%	12.6%	13.2%	11.9%

Tax administration

An important factor to consider when assessing whether a tax system meets the transparency, neutrality and low marginal rates rules is its administration and maintenance, which should be kept to a minimum. Tax should be predictable and stable to minimise the marginal rates necessary for a given revenue target. To achieve this aim, the government should publish a formal tax strategy, index all thresholds, end tax policy announcements in annual budgets, subject all tax policy decisions to dynamic scoring, improve monitoring and analysis of tax expenditures, and advise taxpayers of details of any tax they have paid.

Formal tax strategy

A formal tax strategy that expresses the government's medium- and long-term intentions should be published to provide tax-payers and policymakers with a framework for the overall direction for any future changes in the system. This should reduce uncertainty and improve the coherence of decision-making. The government should commit itself to stating how every change in tax policy adheres to the strategy and explain why the strategy is being contravened where it is necessary to do so.

Threshold indexation

A good tax system should retain a minimum number of thresholds, but those which do remain should be indexed to the appropriate index to ensure the thresholds meet their aims with the minimum of intervention and uncertainty. For example, income tax thresholds should be indexed to average incomes and Pigovian taxes should be indexed to measures of the externalised harm.

Annual budgets

Tax policy decision-making should be taken out of budgets and implemented separately from periodic statements involving economic and fiscal forecasting so that fuller attention can be devoted to the implications of both tax policy changes and changes in budgetary and economic forecasts, respectively. Tax policy changes should not be announced within a week of a periodic statement of accounts unless there is an unavoidable emergency that cannot wait.

Full dynamic scoring

HMRC developed a computable general equilibrium model which was used to analyse recent cuts in the main rate of corporation tax, providing the Treasury with a fuller (yet still incomplete) analysis of the dynamic effects of tax policy changes on revenues. This has obvious consequences for the transparency of the system and meeting the low marginal rates rule. Dynamic modelling should be further developed and its use should be applied to all proposed changes to tax policy.

Tax expenditure monitoring

A good tax system should retain as few exemptions, thresholds and rates as possible to adhere to the transparency, neutrality and low marginal rates rules. While tax exemptions or targeted cuts are not the same as spending measures, they often have substantially equivalent effects on incentives, distortions and outcomes. The negative impact of the tax system on taxpayers is not limited to the cash value confiscated. It also arises from the incentives a system creates which distort decision-making by economic agents. This distortionary welfare loss can be as much of a problem for a tax break as it is for equivalent spending programmes. Tax breaks that remain should be subject to close monitoring to ensure that they continue to meet their objectives and the aims of the government's tax strategy.

Tax transparency

Tax should be made as transparent as possible. Where possible, the legal incidence of tax should lie with those who bear the economic incidence. Where this is not possible, those who bear the economic burden should be kept informed. For example, employee remuneration slips should include a total for wages that includes employer's national insurance contributions, which should also be included in the entry for the employee's total tax figure. Similarly, price labels and till receipts should include the taxes charged to purchases.

REFERENCES

Alloza, M. (2016) *The Impact of Taxes on Income Mobility*. London: University College London.

Arnold, J. (2008) *Do Tax Structures Affect Aggregate Economic Growth? Empirical Evidence from a Panel of OECD Countries* (available at http://www.oecd.org/officialdocuments/publicdisplaydocument pdf/?doclanguage=en&cote=eco/wkp%282008%2951). OECD Economics Department Working Paper 643. Paris: OECD Publishing.

Blöchliger, H. (2013) Decentralisation and economic growth. Part 1. How fiscal federalism affects long-term development. Working Papers on Fiscal Federalism 14. Paris: OECD.

Booth, P. (2015) *Federal Britain: The Case for Decentralisation*. Readings in Political Economy 3. London: Institute of Economic Affairs.

Bourne, R. (2014) *Taxing Problem: The UK's Incoherent Tax System*, briefing 14:09. London: Institute of Economic Affairs.

Buser, W. (2011) The impact of fiscal decentralization on economics performance in high-income OECD nations: an institutional approach. *Public Choice* 149: 31–48.

Gemmell, N., Kneller, R. and Sanz, I. (2013) Fiscal decentralization and economic growth: spending versus revenue decentralization. *Economic Inquiry* 51: 1915–31.

Heath, A. et al. (2012) *The Single Income Tax*. London: 2020 Tax Commission. The TaxPayers' Alliance and the Institute of Directors.

Herring, S. (2015) *GE2015: The IoD's Key Priorities for Tax Reforms*. London: Institute of Directors.

Keable-Elliott, I. and Papworth, T. (2015) *Unbiased Capital: Making Tax Work for Business*. London: Centre Forum.

Lawton, K. and Reed, H. (2013) *Property and Wealth Taxes in the UK: The Context for Reform*. London: Institute for Public Policy Research.

Mankiw, N., Weinzierl, M. and Yagan, D. (2009) Optimal taxation in theory and practice. *Journal of Economic Perspectives* 23(4): 147–74.

Manning, W. G., Blumberg, L. and Moulton, L. H. (1995) The demand for alcohol: the differential response to price. *Journal of Health Economics* 14: 123–48.

Meakin, R. (2012) Make it simple. *Taxation* 169(4358): 6–8.

Mirrlees, J., Adam, S., Besley, T., Blundell, R., Bond, S., Chote, R., Gammie, M., Johnson, P., Myles, G. and Poterba, J. (2011) *Tax by Design*. London: Institute for Fiscal Studies.

OECD (2010) *Tax Policy Reform and Economic Growth*. OECD Tax Policy Studies no. 20. Paris: OECD Publishing.

Packer, T. and Sinclair, M. (2015) *Slicing up the Public Sector*. London: Institute for Economic Affairs.

Saatchi, M. (2014) *The Road from Serfdom*. London: Centre for Policy Studies.

Smith, A. (1776) *An Inquiry into the Nature and Causes of the Wealth of Nations* (ed. S. Soares, 2007). MetaLibri Digital Library.

Stern, N. (2006) *Stern Review on the Economics of Climate Change*. London: HM Treasury.

US Environmental Protection Agency (2016) *GHG Equivalencies Calculator – Calculations and References* (https://www.epa.gov/energy/ghg-equivalencies-calculator-calculations-and-references – accessed 14 June 2016).

Wellings, R. (2012) *Time to Excise Fuel Duty?* Current Controversies 39. London: Institute of Economic Affairs.

ABOUT THE IEA

The Institute is a research and educational charity (No. CC 235 351), limited by guarantee. Its mission is to improve understanding of the fundamental institutions of a free society by analysing and expounding the role of markets in solving economic and social problems.

The IEA achieves its mission by:

- a high-quality publishing programme
- conferences, seminars, lectures and other events
- outreach to school and college students
- brokering media introductions and appearances

The IEA, which was established in 1955 by the late Sir Antony Fisher, is an educational charity, not a political organisation. It is independent of any political party or group and does not carry on activities intended to affect support for any political party or candidate in any election or referendum, or at any other time. It is financed by sales of publications, conference fees and voluntary donations.

In addition to its main series of publications the IEA also publishes a quarterly journal, *Economic Affairs*.

The IEA is aided in its work by a distinguished international Academic Advisory Council and an eminent panel of Honorary Fellows. Together with other academics, they review prospective IEA publications, their comments being passed on anonymously to authors. All IEA papers are therefore subject to the same rigorous independent refereeing process as used by leading academic journals.

IEA publications enjoy widespread classroom use and course adoptions in schools and universities. They are also sold throughout the world and often translated/reprinted.

Since 1974 the IEA has helped to create a worldwide network of 100 similar institutions in over 70 countries. They are all independent but share the IEA's mission.

Views expressed in the IEA's publications are those of the authors, not those of the Institute (which has no corporate view), its Managing Trustees, Academic Advisory Council members or senior staff.

Members of the Institute's Academic Advisory Council, Honorary Fellows, Trustees and Staff are listed on the following page.

The Institute gratefully acknowledges financial support for its publications programme and other work from a generous benefaction by the late Professor Ronald Coase.

Other books recently published by the IEA include:

The Future of the Commons – Beyond Market Failure and Government Regulation
Elinor Ostrom et al.
Occasional Paper 148; ISBN 978-0-255-36653-3; £10.00

Redefining the Poverty Debate – Why a War on Markets Is No Substitute for a War on Poverty
Kristian Niemietz
Research Monograph 67; ISBN 978-0-255-36652-6; £12.50

The Euro – the Beginning, the Middle … and the End?
Edited by Philip Booth
Hobart Paperback 39; ISBN 978-0-255-36680-9; £12.50

The Shadow Economy
Friedrich Schneider & Colin C. Williams
Hobart Paper 172; ISBN 978-0-255-36674-8; £12.50

Quack Policy – Abusing Science in the Cause of Paternalism
Jamie Whyte
Hobart Paper 173; ISBN 978-0-255-36673-1; £10.00

Foundations of a Free Society
Eamonn Butler
Occasional Paper 149; ISBN 978-0-255-36687-8; £12.50

The Government Debt Iceberg
Jagadeesh Gokhale
Research Monograph 68; ISBN 978-0-255-36666-3; £10.00

A U-Turn on the Road to Serfdom
Grover Norquist
Occasional Paper 150; ISBN 978-0-255-36686-1; £10.00

New Private Monies – A Bit-Part Player?
Kevin Dowd
Hobart Paper 174; ISBN 978-0-255-36694-6; £10.00

From Crisis to Confidence – Macroeconomics after the Crash
Roger Koppl
Hobart Paper 175; ISBN 978-0-255-36693-9; £12.50

Advertising in a Free Society
Ralph Harris and Arthur Seldon
With an introduction by Christopher Snowdon
Hobart Paper 176; ISBN 978-0-255-36696-0; £12.50

Selfishness, Greed and Capitalism: Debunking Myths about the Free Market
Christopher Snowdon
Hobart Paper 177; ISBN 978-0-255-36677-9; £12.50

Waging the War of Ideas
John Blundell
Occasional Paper 131; ISBN 978-0-255-36684-7; £12.50

Brexit: Directions for Britain Outside the EU
Ralph Buckle, Tim Hewish, John C. Hulsman, Iain Mansfield and Robert Oulds
Hobart Paperback 178; ISBN 978-0-255-36681-6; £12.50

Flaws and Ceilings – Price Controls and the Damage They Cause
Edited by Christopher Coyne and Rachel Coyne
Hobart Paperback 179; ISBN 978-0-255-36701-1; £12.50

Scandinavian Unexceptionalism: Culture, Markets and the Failure of Third-Way Socialism
Nima Sanandaji
Readings in Political Economy 1; ISBN 978-0-255-36704-2; £10.00

Classical Liberalism – A Primer
Eamonn Butler
Readings in Political Economy 2; ISBN 978-0-255-36707-3; £10.00

Federal Britain: The Case for Decentralisation
Philip Booth
Readings in Political Economy 3; ISBN 978-0-255-36713-4; £10.00

Forever Contemporary: The Economics of Ronald Coase
Edited by Cento Veljanovski
Readings in Political Economy 4; ISBN 978-0-255-36710-3; £15.00

Power Cut? How the EU Is Pulling the Plug on Electricity Markets
Carlo Stagnaro
Hobart Paperback 180; ISBN 978-0-255-36716-5; £10.00

Policy Stability and Economic Growth – Lessons from the Great Recession
John B. Taylor
Readings in Political Economy 5; ISBN 978-0-255-36719-6; £7.50

Breaking Up Is Hard To Do: Britain and Europe's Dysfunctional Relationship
Edited by Patrick Minford and J. R. Shackleton
Hobart Paperback 181; ISBN 978-0-255-36722-6; £15.00

In Focus: The Case for Privatising the BBC
Edited by Philip Booth
Hobart Paperback 182; ISBN 978-0-255-36725-7; £12.50

Islamic Foundations of a Free Society
Edited by Nouh El Harmouzi and Linda Whetstone
Hobart Paperback 183; ISBN 978-0-255-36728-8; £12.50

The Economics of International Development: Foreign Aid versus Freedom for the World's Poor
William Easterly
Readings in Political Economy 6; ISBN 978-0-255-36731-8; £7.50

Other IEA publications

Comprehensive information on other publications and the wider work of the IEA can be found at www.iea.org.uk. To order any publication please see below.

Personal customers

Orders from personal customers should be directed to the IEA:

Clare Rusbridge
IEA
2 Lord North Street
FREEPOST LON10168
London SW1P 3YZ
Tel: 020 7799 8907. Fax: 020 7799 2137
Email: sales@iea.org.uk

Trade customers

All orders from the book trade should be directed to the IEA's distributor:

NBN International (IEA Orders)
Orders Dept.
NBN International
10 Thornbury Road
Plymouth PL6 7PP
Tel: 01752 202301, Fax: 01752 202333
Email: orders@nbninternational.com

IEA subscriptions

The IEA also offers a subscription service to its publications. For a single annual payment (currently £42.00 in the UK), subscribers receive every monograph the IEA publishes. For more information please contact:

Clare Rusbridge
Subscriptions
IEA
2 Lord North Street
FREEPOST LON10168
London SW1P 3YZ
Tel: 020 7799 8907, Fax: 020 7799 2137
Email: crusbridge@iea.org.uk